Leadership and learning are indispensable to each other.

– John F. Kennedy

Knowledge is only rumor until it lives in the bones.

– Asaro Tribe Saying

LIFE AS A LEADER

A PRACTICAL GUIDE TO MASTERY IN COMMUNICATION, WORKPLACE RELATIONSHIPS, AND BUILDING TEAMS

Marimac

JONES MEDIA
PUBLISHING

Jones Media Publishing
10645 N. Tatum Blvd. Ste. 200-166
Phoenix, AZ 85028
www.JonesMediaPublishing.com

Disclaimer:

The author strives to be as accurate and complete as possible in the creation of this book, notwithstanding the fact that the author does not warrant or represent at any time that the contents within are accurate due to the rapidly changing nature of the Internet.

While all attempts have been made to verify information provided in this publication, the Author and Publisher assume no responsibility and are not liable for errors, omissions, or contrary interpretation of the subject matter herein. The Author and Publisher hereby disclaim any liability, loss or damage incurred as a result of the application and utilization, whether directly or indirectly, of any information, suggestion, advice, or procedure in this book. Any perceived slights of specific persons, peoples, or organizations are unintentional.

In practical advice books, like anything else in life, there are no guarantees of income made. Readers are cautioned to rely on their own judgment about their individual circumstances to act accordingly. Readers are responsible for their own actions, choices, and results. This book is not intended for use as a source of legal, business, accounting or financial advice. All readers are advised to seek services of competent professionals in legal, business, accounting, and finance field.

Printed in the United States of America

ISBN-13: 978-1-945849-82-4 paperback
JMP2019.9

DEDICATION

THIS BOOK IS dedicated to the two most important men in
my life. They have always believed in me, saved me from
myself, and so many other things.
All my love and devotion!

Marc & Will

CONTENTS

AUTHOR'S NOTE

IN THE COURSE of writing this book, I included many stories of my personal experience. While not all the stories are positive, I am grateful for all the experiences. I would not be who I am today without them. I did my best to be authentic in my experiences. This is not meant to represent fact, but my own point of view of situations I experienced. These stories are many years old and as such have relied on my memory alone to describe the situation and in some cases exaggerated to illustrate a point.

ACKNOWLEDGEMENTS

THANK YOU TO everyone who has been and will be a part of my continued journey to be my best self. In particular, I would like to thank the following people for their support and encouragement: Anita Dolliver: Leyla Christopher; Janis Chastain; Tony Drake; Chris Bennett; Sue Goetz; Tandra Wiley; Kathy O'Brien; Jim Morrison; Emily Ann Taylor; Gillian Goodman; Tracy Fettig; Dean McMann; and Cortney Doleson.

★　　★　　★

FINALLY, I WOULD like to thank Brene' Brown for her spiritual awakening, stepping into the arena in full force, and her campaign for courage – she changed my life forever!

~ 1 ~
THE IMPETUS

YOU ARE A leader! Yes, YOU!

Everyone leads something, whether it is your own life, a team, a department, a company, a church, a family, or a small group. There are countless books available related to leadership. The first question you may be asking yourself is, *what will this book do for me?* Time is a gift, so I aim to answer this question completely and directly in this first chapter.

Life as a Leader is a conversation between you and me. This is not a lengthy personal tale or biography but rather a collection of short excerpts from my life that I hope you find humorous, insightful, and eye opening. I pair my stories with the practical, research- and experience-based findings I have learned along the way. None of this information is new, per se, to the coaching world, but this book reinforces the research you would find in many other leadership books. Consider my candid tales proof that the recommendations do work.

Below is a concise list of what you'll discover and take with you from this armchair coach, not only into your job but also into your entire life:

- You will learn what it means to be a warrior in the arena versus a critic in the stands.

- As a leader, you will discover techniques for how to engage others, get results, and love the work you do.
- *Life as a Leader* will inspire you to show up as you.
- *Life as a Leader* is different because it doesn't just tell you how to lead; it shows you how to lead by equipping you with strategies through a mixture of storytelling and sound coaching advice.
- You will learn how humility and honest storytelling can transform your ability to understand some of the leadership advice you already know.

★   ★   ★

My first experience with a formal leadership role was as a Chief Financial Officer (CFO). Yes, you read that correctly–no middle management experience and no climb up the proverbial ladder. I was thrown right into the fire. Being a twenty-something woman at that level of a job in the mid-1990s was less than easy. I share this with you because there is a responsibility that comes with leadership that has nothing to do with the job we're filling or the people we are. It's bigger than those things. The responsibility of a leader is to set the tone, manage expectations, and understand our influence. It's more than a rung on the ladder. As businessman Peter Drucker said, "Rank does not confer privilege or give power. It imposes responsibility."

How we show up in our roles and own the responsibility that comes with it defines us as leaders. My role as CFO is where I learned this particular truth the hard way.

I was young, proud, and a bit arrogant–a rebel. As the new CFO, I walked into a mess. It was a hospital business going down the drain. With each passing cycle, there were worries that payroll might not be met, our relationships with major vendors had been severed, and we were ninety days in arrears with our payments. It was a nightmare. My job description, according to the Chief Executive Officer (CEO), was to be the "bad guy" to offset his "good guy" reputation. For clarity, I asked him to outline my specific responsibilities, and he pulled out an organizational chart. He pointed to his role and said, "good guy" and then pointed to my new job title and said, "bad guy." And, so it began.

Some may think it was brave (or stupid) of me to take on this job, and in hindsight it probably was both brave and stupid, but I had my eyes set on more financial security and, of course, success.

In order to save this particular business–and save it, I did–I had to lead the charge toward a full turnaround within eighteen months time. However, that is not what this story is about. This story is about failure at the hands of bravery.

At this point in my life, I had no emotional intelligence, or emotional quotient as it is measured (EQ). Our EQ describes our ability to monitor our own emotions and the emotions of others. Emotional intelligence allows us to distinguish between and label emotions correctly. The greater the EQ, the more capacity we have to use this emotional information to guide our thinking and behaviors. In my professional infancy and with my lack of management training, I did not fully understand my impact on others or appreciate the consequences of my words and actions. Because of my bravery, I left many people feeling disheartened, sad, and even angry. In retrospect, I felt a bit like Tom Hanks in the movie *Big*, trying to discern mature ideas well before my capacity to do so was developed.

During my time as CFO, I received a late night phone call at home from the Director of Nursing at the hospital. She indicated there was an issue in the emergency department (ED) involving the physician who was working the night shift. It was bad. To say this guy "lost it" would be an understatement. She informed me he had thrown equipment around the ED and wrapped a stethoscope around a nurse's neck.

I asked, "What do you need me to do?" She was exasperated. The Chief of Staff would not take action to send the doctor home, the CEO was unreachable, and unbeknownst to me at the time, I was the next one on the call list to make a decision.

At this revelation, my internal monologue was fit for a sailor. *What the f*ck? Are you kidding me?* (Fair warning: This book is about showing up as you to lead well. I aim to do the same. I am direct. I am honest. And I will cuss.) I asked her the urgent questions: "Is the nurse okay? Does she need medical treatment? Has an incident report been written up? Do we have a back-up on-call doc who can cover the ED tonight?" I had parallel questions running through my mind as well. *Do I need to call the attorney? Should we close the ED and divert patients to another hospital until morning?*

You see my bravery–my "overdeveloped sense of fight"–served me well during crises. I became hyper-focused and went into problem-solving mode, especially when I was not directly involved in any personal threat (perceived or real).

I made the decision to send the doctor home and closed the ED until morning. To this day, I stand behind that decision. It was the right one for the safety of all involved. However, a Board of Directors meeting was scheduled shortly afterwards. The Board wanted to hold me accountable for making a decision the rest of the physicians on staff did not support. (The notion of MDs protecting MDs is all too real, folks.)

I stood just inside the boardroom, sweating that nervous sweat and feeling very much like someone was going to hurt me. I wondered if I would be fired or suspended. I didn't know what to expect, but one thing was clear: I was alone in a room filled with angry doctors and a Board of Directors who seemed to be on their side. I now perceived a personal threat.

I sat down and laid out my case. I don't remember much of what I said. However, I will never forget these words of mine: "It was clear this MD had lost it, and it was no longer safe for him to treat patients. I do not believe we should further employ this physician, due to the risk he poses to employees and patients. Clearly, throwing medical equipment around an ED and physically assaulting a nurse...He was out of control, and we don't need the risk." This seemed obvious to me. I expected to get some level of support from at least the administrative team and the attorney. I was wrong.

One of the MDs (not the chief, but an informal leader) barked at me, "You are not a physician! You are not qualified to determine if someone is unfit to work or has any sort of mental impairment." When I perceive a personal threat, I fight back–hard. I used to tell people, "Don't back me in a corner. I bite."

I did not read the room well or understand the politics at play. At this point, everything went from bad to worse. My response was disrespectful, threatening, and though not entirely wrong, it was not right either.

"I am not a proctologist, but I know an asshole when I see one. If this group of people, who are responsible for the health and well-being of this community we serve, is not willing to take a stand when one of your own breaks the code of conduct, this will get very ugly for all of you. If the situation involved two employees [rather than a physician and a nurse], you would not hesitate to intervene and fire the individual involved. So, take the action you know is right, or I will go to the press."

Clearly, my reaction was not diplomatic, based in partnership, or even courageous. I had failed to pause and think about the impact of my words on myself or the other people in the room. That first condescending sentence and the threats contained in my reply were absolutely unnecessary. (Although, you should know that going to the press was not a threat, as I would have done that in a second.) However, what the physicians felt in that room was an insult to their profession and to them personally. It was not my proudest moment, and it began a course of repercussions that eventually resulted in me leaving.

Throughout this book, I will share personal and vulnerable stories– like this one– alongside practical lessons for becoming a strong and trusted leader. The lesson here is:

When you choose your time to stand, be brave, respectful, and listen with an open mind.

I knew I was rebellious from the get-go. Even as a child, I toed outside the boundary lines and skirted past ordinary. I grew up as the oldest of four children–three girls and a boy. I cannot pinpoint from where my desire to be a leader came. It was not a time when that was encouraged in girls, yet I seemed to be a natural one.

I was born with a chronic illness, which I must continue to manage for the rest of my life. This has contributed to my views in many ways. Some of these perspectives were extremely helpful to my career while others seemed to get in the way, at least until I could understand them more fully. With my illness, I spent many hours as a child in bed with my thoughts. One of the more recurring topics I contemplated was my own mortality. Even at a young age, I wondered about life, death, and the timing of it all. Being intermittently bed-ridden and lost within these hefty reflections impacted me a lot. It didn't take long for me to become somewhat socially awkward. Those occasions when I was well enough to join in social activities, I didn't always feel like I belonged.

I have also been brave for as long as I can remember. My propensity for standing up to authority is just one of the ways my bravery spills out. In my youth and as a young adult, my bravery meant having that "overdeveloped sense of fight" as I managed crises.

I was brave, but I also understood my place as a child. I respected my parents. I just did not always submit to their wishes. As the oldest child in my family, I grew up feeling the pressure of being responsible for my siblings. As a rebel, I did what I could to find my independence. One of those places was in school. I valued good grades but rarely received them. I'm not sure if it was because I struggled with a learning disability that flew under the radar for much of my life or if it was one more way to live on the opposite side of everybody's expectations. My family valued appearances, so I learned how to comply with societal norms when absolutely necessary, despite my bend toward wayward thoughts, appearances, and choices. Back in the mid-1960s and '70s, those norms included going to church and attending social and family functions, which I did as best I could, given my illness and social angst.

The worries, self-doubt, and uncertainty of my childhood and adolescence followed me into adulthood. Of course, no one likes to live in fear or with hesitation, so anger became my comfortable, fallback emotion. I suppose it was a coping mechanism. When I was angry, I felt powerful. When I was angry, people left me alone.

I went to college straight out of high school for two reasons. First, it was expected of me. Second, I was ready to move forward and be completely independent. I was not thrilled about the prospect of more studying and formal education, however I was captivated with architecture. I decided to declare it as my major as it suited my creative mind. I devoted myself to compiling my best work for the required portfolio and application.

The university to which I applied loved my portfolio but certainly not my grades. The decision makers offered a compromise that would allow me to enter the architecture school a semester later, once I successfully completed a few general courses to improve my Grade Point Average (GPA). It was a fair deal. Nevertheless, I impolitely declined. I felt rejected, and as a result, decided they were in the wrong.

I floundered around in summer school and took some college courses for a short time. Then, I met a man, we became engaged, and I dropped out of school completely. As you can imagine, this was not received well by anyone in my family.

Soon after, I started my career in a hospital. For a number of reasons, when I was younger, I never thought I was very intelligent. I eventually overcame this, but during this early season of my professional journey, the lie that I was somehow not smart enough hindered my progress. I didn't realize that much of the time I was, in fact, one of the most intelligent people in the room. Because of this, I failed to stand out, take risks, or assert my opinions often enough.

A few years later, I applied for a job as a leader. I was told–as many of you may have heard early in your careers–I did not have enough experience or the required degree; therefore, I would not be considered for the role. I felt annoyed and angry because, again, those emotions were easy. They safely covered the regret, disappointment, and rejection I was truly experiencing. In my anger, I thought, *well, I will show you!*

I rationalized away the deep hurt. *What does a degree have to do with anything? It's just a piece of paper.* I decided to focus on broadening my experience, and over the next couple years, I transitioned through two different departments at the hospital.

While I was gaining this experience, leadership roles remained elusive. I finally decided that going back to college was a necessary choice (oxymoron fully intended) if I wanted to venture into higher-level jobs. I did not believe I needed an advanced degree– school wasn't going to teach me anything because...well, it never had. I was not capable of learning that way. I had street smarts and a growing confidence. I knew if I could focus, get through the curriculum, and graduate then new doors would open for me.

At this point, I was earning $6.50 per hour, as was my new husband. Neither of us believed it was wise to leave a job to pursue education. The colleges around us did not have night programs, so I began a campaign to work a flexible schedule to afford me the opportunity to earn my degree while working at my current job. I was met with some resistance from my leader and his director. The conversation unfolded something like this:

"I am going back to college and would like to work a flexible schedule in order to do so." I was displaying so much resourcefulness that I couldn't stand it.

He replied, "You can't go back to college."

My response (as you can imagine by now) was matter-of-fact. "You're confused. I am going back to college; it is just a matter of if I continue to work here while I do it."

I didn't make a lot of money, but I was really good at what I did. At this point, I did not understand that he didn't want to lose me. I knew I could find another job easily, but I just didn't want to go to the trouble.

The concern was that if they allowed this policy change for me, they would have to allow it for everyone. I indicated I would go "up" to discuss the request further, but my leader suggested he would do so. He came back to me a second time with the same answer, and again, I informed him I would go up the ladder to plead my case. I was relentless. He said he and his director would try to handle it.

Some time later, my leader sat down with me and shared the good news–we could create a flexible schedule so that I could return to school. The story goes that the CFO's rationalization was this: "I don't think everyone will want to do this; it is not an easy thing to do–working full time and being a full-time student. Even if others wanted to pursue it, why would that be a bad thing?" This was a transformative moment in my career.

After years of hesitation, I was returning to college. I chose the field of accounting. Unbeknownst to me, that same CFO who paved the way for my opportunity took a further interest in what I was doing and followed my progress from his own vantage point. Consequently, he became my mentor.

A couple of years later, I proudly earned my Bachelor of Science degree. I sidled into his office to present him with an invitation to my graduation in appreciation for his ongoing support. He accepted the invitation and inquired, "What do you want to do now?"

"Well, your job looks pretty good," I replied in my notoriously direct and fiery style. He smiled, and challenged me with a question.

"So what are you missing?"

I sat down. He had generously offered his time, and we talked about what I needed to do to elevate my experience profile to attain a job as a CFO. It was a productive conversation but one I took as coaching rather than as an interview.

Meanwhile, I made preparations to sit for the CPA exam. Before the exam, I attended a networking gathering, otherwise known as my favorite thing in the world–a social event, held by the Big 8. (It may help to note that the largest accounting firms were referred to as the Big 8 up until 1989.)

Despite my tendencies toward social awkwardness, I was excited for this event. I felt it would be a major step forward in my pursuit of the leadership role for which I had been dreaming and working. It was time for me to prove to myself–and quite possibly my parents, mentor, and others–that I was more than capable.

I was pleased with the new outfit I had purchased for the event. It was a teal suit and a pair of fantastic shoes. Lifting my chin with confidence, I walked those fashionable shoes and bright suit into the room and right into a sea of black, beige, and navy. I gaped at the amount of neutral tones. Immediately and instinctively, I knew I didn't belong. It was not an insecurity resurfacing, but it was the first time I began questioning my current career path of accounting. I turned around, and walked back out of the event, disappointed that perhaps I was on the wrong track with my professional pursuits. I never sat for the CPA exam.

My mentor continued to provide me with opportunities that pointed me in the one direction I felt certain I wanted to grow–toward a leadership role. I worked with several senior level executives on projects at the hospital until one day a new venture emerged.

After years of hard work, networking, and building my experience and education profiles, I was tagged to become the controller for a new nursing home. The CFO, my mentor, had been grooming me for this. To say I was excited would have been an understatement.

Days later, my husband informed me that we were moving. I couldn't believe it. I was sorely disappointed, but we left. I was twenty-seven years old, but I knew exactly what I wanted in our new city. I still had not fully accepted the unrest I felt at that earth-toned networking event, so I set a goal of landing an accounting job earning thirty thousand dollars per year. My mentor was kind enough to write an armful of recommendation letters to all the hospitals in the area to which we moved, endorsing me for any jobs they might have available.

Nothing transpired right away. During one particular consultation at the unemployment office, the woman conducting the interview asked, "Can you type?"

"No, and I don't need to because I am an accountant."

"Women aren't accountants here in this neck of the woods. You're not from around

here, are you?" Her reply sent a ripple of anger through my core. I pushed back and informed her I would be an accountant and my salary requirement was thirty thousand dollars. Laughing, she explained my expectations were unreasonable.

Despite this unprofessional and prejudiced slap to my psyche–to all career women's psyches–I did get a job in accounting. In fact, despite the lack of management experience on my resume, a hospital CEO offered me that role of Chief Financial Officer where my first story in this book started.

A couple years went by. Then after a divorce, a few job changes, obtaining my Master of Business Administration (MBA) and Project

Management Professional certification (PMP), I found myself working at what is today a Fortune 100 Company. I spent a number of years working directly with clients and building a name for myself. I was invited to customer summits and was included on stage with my customers when they won awards. This was a first for the company. As is typical for high performers, I was eventually asked to run a team. Though hesitant, I finally agreed when the president called me at home early one morning to tell me I was the only person who could do the job. My ego had been stroked. Throughout my career, I had not received any formal leadership training. In fact, I had never been a front line leader–always an executive. While that may sound impressive, it did not serve me well.

None of us go to school for the soft skills of leadership: flexibility, humility, building trust, self-reflection, and performance acknowledgement, to name a few. Imitation may be the sincerest form of flattery, yet it is one of the most dangerous forms of self-denial. I had many mentors throughout my career, and I learned to mimic those leaders around me sitting at the executive tables. These mentors, peers, and leaders were always men, so I learned to emulate male leaders rather than embrace the strengths I offered as a female leader. Over time, I came to understand–the hard way–that as a woman, emulating those behaviors, while perfectly acceptable coming from male executives, was completely intolerable coming from me–whether I was with men or other women. I should have been taming my confidence and showing more of my true self, while demonstrating my compassion, kindness, and ability to bring innovative solutions to the table. While these are not only female strengths (there are many men who have these skills and some women who don't), these were the specific traits I could have been using to build my reputation as a leader.

I spent seventeen years with the Fortune 100 Company, weaving my way through a number of roles. This is the advantage of working in a large corporation–the diversity of opportunities available to employees without having to leave the company. The disadvantage is that all one's experience is gained through the same culture and narrow point of view.

Unfortunately, I hit a ceiling. I could easily blame the usual suspect– the best jobs were being offered to the males. While true, I also played a role in the sudden stop in my upward mobility. I didn't actually see it that way until I left, but the specifics of that story are for another time and perhaps another book. For now, let's just say that one employee opinion survey changed everything about how I chose to lead going forward. I did a number of things to get to the heart of the issues these individuals had raised–employee round tables, employee action committees, and intentional communication. Eventually, with the help of my human resources partner, we got to the root of the issue. It boiled down to one area: trust. I will address trust and rapport later in this book.

As with all large corporations, there was a reorganization, and I was scooped up by someone at another organization who was a fan, and I was able to find my way again. It was a struggle, but by the time I left, I had earned a seat at the senior executive table, reporting to the president. The company was sold, and I decided not to be a part of the new business. My heart wasn't in it anymore. Over the course of a number of months and after a lot of research, interviews, and more schooling, I concluded that my journey as a leader should move onto the path of helping others be better leaders. After all, I had struggled and prevailed. I knew I had something to offer.

*   *   *

I have been where you now tread. Dare I say–I was you, carrying the mixed bag of sentiments that a leadership role generates. The challenges. The insecurities. The questions. The opportunities. The hope. I know them well.

Everyone is a leader. First and foremost, we all lead our own lives. How we act and communicate affects everyone around us. While this book is published to coach workplace leaders, it was written to elicit change for the leader in all of us. Whether you are a first-time leader or one who is transitioning through the leadership journey into a new role with growing responsibilities, you will find *Living Leadership* to be a valuable resource for laying the foundation for success–your organization's success, your team's success, and your own personal success.

I base the majority of my vision and the strategies to achieve them on this quote from President Roosevelt, taken from his speech in Paris, France at the Sorbonne called "Citizenship in a Republic" on April 23, 1910:

> "It is not the critic who counts; it's not the man who points out how strong man stumbles, or where the doer of deeds could have done them better. The credit belongs to the man who is actually in the arena, whose face is marred by dust and sweat and blood; who strives valiantly; who errs, who comes up short again and again, because there is no effort without error and shortcoming; but who does actually strive to do the deeds; who know great enthusiasms, the great devotions; who spends himself in a worthy cause; who at the best knows in the end the triumph of high achievement, and who at the worst, if

he fails, at least fails while daring greatly, so that his place shall never be with those cold and timid souls who neither know victory nor defeat."

I first read this quote in Brené Brown's book, *Daring Greatly*. This is one of the resources I used to transform my leadership approach and rebuild trust within my teams. I credit Brené's books and research for laying the foundation of my transformation. Her work–as well as those written by others–provided the learning. It took me living it out to become the leader I knew I was capable of being.

As I read the full speech, "Citizenship in a Republic," I knew immediately my journey had just taken a new and exciting turn. To say I was inspired would be an understatement. I pursued additional research and information from behavioral science to numerous leadership studies and white papers. I became an expert in it all, continually asking *why* and *what else,* digging deeper to get past the obvious. I have compiled my best thoughts, stories, and practices. These are my testimonies that all the research, guidelines, and recommendations out there really do work. I have a special note to make, however. Sometimes in my metaphorical references or while providing recommendations, I often speak from an obviously female perspective. For example, I may refer to a warrior as either "he" or "she" throughout the book. I am a woman and it's not meant to ostracize you male leaders. This book is for everyone.

I can't wait to share this with you so you can learn how to *live the learning* as well. But first, what–or where–is this arena?

~ 2 ~
THE ROMAN COLOSSEUM

PRESIDENT THEODORE ROOSEVELT's famous quote from his speech, "Citizenship in a Republic," positions us in the arena. What is the arena? For me, the quote summoned images of gladiators and transported me specifically to the famous Roman Colosseum– which happened to be a feat of architectural ingenuity for its time. The structure was built using travertine and brick-faced cement between the years 72 and 80 A.D. It was constructed after the death of Nero and during several emperors' reigns, yet all within one dynasty, the Flavian dynasty, as a gift to the Roman people. The Colosseum was actually not built by the Romans but by their slaves, and it was erected, in part, to showcase Rome's engineering skills to the world.

Initially, I struggled with the imagery of a man fighting in the arena. It produced two main challenges. Let's get them out of the way, as I assume several of you may have the same hurdles to overcome.

First, there is the violent history correlated with the Colosseum. The structure was home to savage events, including battles to the death between gladiators, animals, and criminals. If the ultimate message within this book is how to propel your dreams of authentic and successful leadership into reality, we can all perhaps agree fighting is counter-productive to that goal. However these battles were not the only form of entertainment at the Roman Colosseum. Additionally, it accommodated plays based on Classical mythology, festivals, speeches, poetry readings, animal circus acts, and reenactments of famous sea battles of the time. Having explained this, it is still imperative that we understand we are in battle as leaders, even if they are mostly inner battles. We can no longer focus solely on ourselves. We have to realize we are now tasked with meeting the needs of others, motivating people, and leading our teams into greatness.

The second mental obstacle I overcame was my assumption that gladiators were all men. Obviously, this is not the case in leadership, so the metaphor could quickly tumble down a steep hill of sexism, effectively negating some of the strategies and insights I will be uncovering in later chapters. During my research, I discovered gladiators were not only men. A gladiatrix is the modern term used for the female equivalent of the gladiator of ancient Rome. Like their male counterparts, gladiatrices fought each other or wild animals to entertain audiences at various games and festivals within the Colosseum and surrounding venues. Very little is known about these gladiatrices. The audiences likely considered these rare clashes to be special affairs. Their existence is acknowledged only through a limited number of accounts marked by members of Rome's ruling class.

If we move past the traditional assumptions of the Colosseum, forgive the gender-specific language of both ancient Rome and President Roosevelt's time, and capture the powerful message of his famous speech through an all-inclusive lens, the metaphor becomes a meaningful one for our purposes. It is a commentary of the times and as such, doesn't negate the message.

The Roman Colosseum was the largest arena ever built at the time of its completion. In fact, it was designed as two Roman theaters that were meshed together to create the whole stadium. Roman law determined where people sat in the Colosseum. The best seats were reserved for the Senators. Behind them were the equestrians or ranking government officials. A bit higher up sat the ordinary Roman citizens (men) and the soldiers. Finally, at the top of the stadium sat the women and behind them, the slaves. The Colosseum held over 50,000 people, and the viewing public was well taken care of by the authorities overseeing the events. In fact, most events were free, and the government graciously fed the attendees in the hopes of keeping them content with ancient Roman life.

The Colosseum had eighty entrances—four main entrances; one used exclusively by royalty and the upper class, two for regular city- and townsfolk, and one reserved for the criminals and slaves who were escorted to the top tier, placing them the furthest from the entertainment. It started as a three-story structure, but a fourth level was added at a later point.

The warriors used several different weapons in the arena. Interestingly, they wanted the pairs of fighters to be equally matched, so they heavily armored one (which limited his mobility) while not armoring the other at all (which left him agile but defenseless). They had specific names for each weapon, but we can classify them as swords, spears and daggers, shields, and nets. In fact, the weapons themselves were ranked, and as warriors attained increasing levels of victory, they were permitted to use more advanced weapons.

These numbers tumbled around in my head; the jagged edges of my preliminary thoughts soon transformed into smooth and well-defined perceptions about life and leadership. The quantities became what I refer to as numeric imagery, solidifying this metaphor of the Roman Colosseum. 2–3–4. Two theaters. Three Tiers. Four weapons. These features are important as we tie the metaphor into the strategies for becoming the leader you want to be. Let's have a look.

Two Theaters

Two theaters were pushed together to form the largest amphitheater the world has ever seen, and they were brilliantly erected on one common foundation. For our metaphor and my story, these foundational theatres are bravery and authenticity. These are the characteristics of successful leadership that are intertwined into every decision and relationship involved in leadership.

Three Tiers

The original three tiers of the Colosseum represent the three different types of critics we will encounter in the leadership arena. The higher the stands, the more rowdy the critics became in ancient Rome. There were townspeople who heckled the warriors and people who sat and gossiped about the latest societal news as they watched the entertainment in the center of the arena. In a similar fashion, leaders must learn to handle the critics in the workplace. There will be those who judge or argue with our decisions or recommendations. There will be those who chat at the water coolers. How leaders deal with these critics will impact their success in the arena, so we will take a deep dive into understanding these individuals. I'll also provide strategies on how to manage them well.

A FOURTH TIER

The final section of the Colosseum, that fourth level–added years after the initial construction of the Colosseum was completed–housed the slaves. The higher the seat and the further from the action, the ruder the spectator became in his or her disapprovals of the event. It's that way in every arena, isn't it? These are the subset of critics I call the bullies and saboteurs. They blame everything and everyone but themselves for their undesirable positions, and they offer unsolicited opinions and criticism about how to do our jobs better. We'll address these types of critics later in the book.

Only those engaged in the actual events, positioned in the leadership roles, truly know the full measure of the battle. Fighting in the middle of the arena is vastly different than sitting and watching in the stands. Moving into the arena from the stands requires sacrifice, information, resources, and courage. A spectator can't just run out into the arena unprepared and expect to survive. When we are able to close the gap between knowledge, action, and accountability, the closer to success we move.

FOUR WEAPONS

Warriors in the Colosseum had several weapons at their disposal. Ranging from harpoon-like spears to nets, they forged tools used for offensive attacks and defensive maneuvers. Likewise, leaders must forge weapons–tools and skills–in order to be successful in the arena. I have defined the four that I believe are most important for leaders. They are self-mastery, communication mastery, relationship mastery, and team mastery. As we enter the leadership arena, we must learn how to employ these four tools effectively, therefore the bulk of this book will be focused on them.

As the details about the ancient Colosseum came into further focus, I realized it was this metaphor that best explained what had manifested in my own life. All at once, as the proverbial light bulb flashed before me, the pieces came together—my coaching practice, this book, and finally my purpose. Through my journey of self-discovery and establishing my own coaching strategies, born from years of experience *in* and *out* of the arena, I realized I had much to offer other leaders, particularly new leaders and those moving up the ladder into roles with greater responsibility. I was able to appreciate the magnitude of the joy that leadership coaching brings me. I was able to see myself in the arena, in the midst of the battle. I was reminded of the blood, sweat, and tears spilled for my personal and professional development. I even recalled the jeers of my naysayers, the critics, along my journey. It was then that the content of this book materialized.

Fighting to become an influential and successful leader is a battle! If we're not living up to our full potential—whether we're in the workplace or the daily grind of life—we are going to die a slow kind of death. It's called giving in or settling. We are cheating ourselves of our passion and purpose. Not only are we cheating ourselves of our purpose, but we are also cheating the world of the gifts and talents we bring to it.

We put ourselves on the front lines to face our critics for the betterment of our teams (and, yes ourselves) as we become leaders. Very few of us are formally educated in many of the skills of life and leadership. We are not born with every personality trait that would enable us to be successful leaders from day one. But, as you'll discover in the coming chapters, we can learn them. Others—the critics—may view some of these characteristics (bravery, authenticity, patience, kindness, and others) as weaknesses. They are not weaknesses. They are strengths. Brené Brown perhaps said it best when she explained this in an interview with Chase Jarvis in 2014. I'm paraphrasing, but what I learned from her interview is that when we feel vulnerable, we feel it as weakness. When we witness vulnerability in others, we see it as strength. This paradox is fascinating to me. When we embrace something larger than ourselves, when we humble ourselves in pursuit of bravery and authenticity, we will become great.

> "Our deepest fear is not that we are inadequate. Our deepest fear is that we are powerful beyond measure. It is our Light, not our Darkness, that most frightens us."
> (Marianne Williamson)

Unfortunately, our society–in my assessment–has found ways to be afraid, to abandon courage in the face of difficulty or the unknown. We are losing our greatness. We don't seek out fear, and we don't ask for circumstances that may produce fear. However, we live in a society that embraces fear and worry to an extent not previously experienced. It has reached the point where it is nearly palpable. A fear-driven life is a life in which thoughts, decisions, and actions are predominantly motivated by fear, trepidation, or unease. The fears are numerous–the fears of our mortality, injury, failure, rejection, poverty, or being alone. They are impacting our workplaces, our culture, and our lives in alarming ways.

I have a vision for leadership where leaders are confidently developing and engaging with their teams through authentic relationships and eliminating fear-based environments. My mission is to unlock key qualities for success in the leaders of the future. There are multiple disparities, constant trials, and a lack of true understanding about how to effectively navigate our business cultures. I am bringing my stories, in the posture of vulnerability, to help others find their way back into the arena–to find connection, fight the good fight, and change the fear-infused thinking that divides us. Winston Churchill reinforced this idea of choosing courage over fear when he said, "Success is not final; failure is not fatal. It is the courage to continue that counts."

The imagery of the Roman Colosseum is a powerful one. It will take this kind of power and insight–vulnerability and humility–to transcend the challenges we face in our arenas. I want to help prevent an epic collapse of our business and personal culture. My hope is that we–as leaders–learn how to face our critics, fears, and learning development head on, always ready for each battle. For, there will be battles on the journey to successful leadership.

In fact, it will be the journey, not the destination, which defines the outcome. A life well-lived is gauged during the living years. In business, we tend to focus on the end goals. Life has only one endpoint, and it's how we battle to get there that matters most. We battle with different methods, attitudes, and weapons, and the timing of our life's end point will vary. In my coaching practice, I help others understand that, despite what our corporate cultures may model, business should not be so different from life itself. If we engage the full measure of our humanity, tackle obstacles with the journey in mind, and learn from each battle, the destination will become a forgone (and successful!) conclusion.

Leaders fall down. Leaders get their asses kicked. Their hearts are broken and their egos are stomped. Circumstances will render leaders bruised and bloody. As leaders, how do we get back up to re-engage? How do we continue to fight for success when we've used every ounce of energy we had just to stand back up? We've all heard the old adage...fall down seven times; get up eight. *Great, but how do we get back into battle once we're standing?* That's what I aim to show you–how I continue to get back up. In her book *Rising Strong*, Brené Brown talks about rising back up after we're knocked down. *Living Leadership* is my testimony–how I applied all the lessons I've learned and how you can apply them too.

Bravery. Facing our critics. Embracing and implementing the learning. Life is about living. When we give up, we are counted out. So, how do we keep fighting? We show up!

As I sat with the "The Man in the Arena" quote and contemplated the entire message of Roosevelt's full "Citizenship in a Republic" speech, I was able to grasp a simple truth. We, who have the capability and desire, also have the responsibility and obligation to lead. We have countless arenas in our lives. They are the arenas of love, partnership, friendship, family, career, faith, health, attitude, and perspective, to name a few. This book is about my journey in the arenas of leadership, however within all these arenas, there will be personal hurdles we will face. There will be critics in the stands, discounting our efforts. There will be obstacles we must overcome in pursuit of becoming who we were made to be.

And, we were born to be great.

~ 3 ~
THE FOUNDATION OF TWO THEATERS

GREAT STRUCTURES AND great leaders have a common denominator. The foundations on which they are built play a pivotal role in their strength and fortitude. Without a stable foundation, both structures and people will crumble under the pressure of internal or external forces. When lacking certain foundational skills and knowledge, emerging leaders will fail to thrive and support high performing teams, ones in which members feel connected to one another and to the mission of the organization.

The Roman Colosseum had no concrete footings to support the meshing of the two theaters and prevent settling. The columns and levels were erected in an oval shape around the earth itself. Over time, a maze of stone tunnels, pulleys, and ancient elevators were built to create a hidden "basement" under the raised floor of the arena. This space was called the hypogeum, which means "the underground." It was from this faux basement where gladiators, wild animals, circus acts, and props for the numerous plays were transported up from the darkness, through trap doors, and into the light of the arena's main stage.

I imagine those gladiators, gladiatrices, entertainers, and even animals were filled with some measure of fear as they ascended into the arena from the hypogeum. I'm sure they could hear the thunderous roar of the 50,000, smell the results from previous events, and feel their hearts beat wilder as they emerged into the center of the chaos. Fear is a palpable emotion. Sweaty palms, an uptick in our pulse, flushed skin–they all indicate the physical response our bodies have to fear. The intrusive thoughts that swirl among the nerves may include questions like *Who do I think I am to do this? What if I fail? Does anyone have my back or am I alone in this battle?* The fighters in the Colosseum were forced to find the bravery required to overcome their fears and react with intentionality. Their lives depended on it.

Leadership success depends on it, too. The quality of our leadership is directly proportional to how we respond when confronted by our fear. Fear causes one of three natural responses: fight, flee, or freeze. We've heard this before, but I want you take a moment to consider if you've demonstrated all these reactions in your personal and professional arenas.

In the Roman Colosseum, a gladiator must choose to fight. If he doesn't, he surely dies. In our everyday lives, the choice to fight rather than flee or freeze is a more difficult one to make. Though the challenges are vastly different in the workplace, science has shown our bodies and minds cannot comprehend the difference between life and death threats and day-to-day confrontations. As a result, the threat feels the same as what those gladiators and gladiatrices experienced. Many factors play into our decisions about how to respond, and we may have only milliseconds to choose. I firmly believe there is no wrong option, but there are consequences for each choice. Choosing to fight, flee, or freeze is essentially the bravest part of the whole process of decision-making. I have chosen them all, and I want you to learn how to as well. First, however, what does it mean to be brave?

Brave is all at once an adjective, a noun, and a verb. The definitions of brave are numerous:

- ready to face danger or pain (adj.)
- a warrior (n.)
- to endure unpleasant conditions or behavior without showing fear (v.)

Bravery is one of those words that elicit strong emotional responses from those who witness its manifestation. Some run from it. Others strive for it. Some model it, while others worry about having to be it. Synonyms of brave include bold, fearless, daring, courageous, audacious, heroic, and plucky. To be brave is to endure, suffer, bear, and weather difficulties. To be called a brave is a label of honor, yet it requires sacrifice. The sacrifice can be significant—great enough that some people are not willing to give that much of themselves. While fear is not inherently bad (it can be an important motivator for self-protection), fear acting apart from wisdom and truth can cloud our judgments, paralyze our forward progress, and hinder our relationships.

Is there a difference between courage and bravery? Despite them being listed as synonyms in most dictionaries, I believe there is a distinct one. Bravery is rash. It's impulsive. Bravery is an immediate response to a fear stimulus. Others may witness bravery's outcomes and call them crazy. True bravery draws no forethought about consequences. From the Italian word "bravo," bravery is based in impulsivity and interestingly, is often portrayed as a more masculine word. On the other hand, courage requires careful thought. It stems from the French word *corage* which means wholeheartedness. Courage is a community-based word, often more feminine in nature, as it relates to our innermost feelings. Courage is planned well in advance; it doesn't just happen. Courage is groomed.

Leadership in all areas of life requires bravery–in-the-moment responses to sudden circumstances. Leadership also requires courage. However, our brave acts are where we can falter the most–those moments of impulsivity rooted in fear or anger. This book is not meant to simply teach us how to be brave. I want us to embrace our strengths, harness bravery, and ultimately develop the courage to be ourselves, no matter what fears we must battle.

Whether we act bravely or are a brave [warrior], we likely experience anxiety or doubt each day. Our society is ensnared in more fear today than in past decades. Recent studies show that the American Fear Index (AFI) is at an all-time high. AFI is the percentage of all news stories during a given time period that contain at least one of four fear-related keywords: fear, risk, danger, or threat. The research indicates that the average AFI score for issues such as war, terror, murder, politics, and natural disasters was 120% higher in 2017 (one year removed from the initial writing of this book) compared to 2016 and 278% higher for 2017 when compared to the historical averages dating back to 1981.

Perhaps our fear-laden culture is the result of the September 11 attacks and the current era of global terror. It may have originated earlier, with the assassinations of Martin Luther King, Jr., John F. Kennedy, and others. Some believe our fear-based society started with the attack on Pearl Harbor in 1941 and has continued to escalate. Still others credit the advancement of technology, the proliferation of online news and media outlets, or the financial collapse of 2008 for impacting the next generations. Valid data on fear only goes back so far, so it's difficult to isolate the turning point, and the statistics are tainted by the culture itself. In fact, fear has become a sort of trend in our world. Peter Stearns, author of *American Fear: The Causes and Consequences of High Anxiety* wrote, "If you think that the society around you expects courage, you may be scared as the dickens but you're not going to say it to a pollster... Currently, fear has become in some ways slightly fashionable, so maybe people are even exaggerating a little bit."

Whatever the origin, there is now a more accepting culture of fear in this country. There are consequences for living in this type of society. Fear can paralyze us into inaction, or we may become content with the status quo. Staying in our current situation–in our comfort zones, if you will–becomes favorable to any forward progress into the unknown. With this paralysis, we render ourselves ineffective.

Almost half (41%) of employees from a range of industries have experienced high levels of anxiety in the workplace. It's a generalized statistic with no objective numbers about what "high levels" means, but it's an interesting piece of information nonetheless. Scott Steinberg, bestselling author of *Make Change Work for You*, cites research in his book regarding the seven most common types of fear people report feeling in the workplace. In no particular order, they are the fears of failure, embarrassment, underperformance, rejection, change and uncertainty, confrontation, and isolation. According to Steinberg, these fears not only hinder personal and team development, but they can snuff out creativity, innovation, and overall business growth as well.

Fear can also cause us to separate into smaller clusters of individuals as a way of self-protection. Typically, these clusters become homogenous as we seek out those who have the same values, thoughts, appearances, and lifestyles we do. This spurs us to focus on the differences between our own smaller groups and the groups around us. These differences lead us to make judgments, and judging is the first step on the road to dehumanizing others.

I believe fear shows up in environments where people are trying to control things that are uncontrollable. This happens frequently in workplace environments and within our relationships. For instance, we cannot control others' personalities, behavior, or reactions. When we try to control others, we create conflict, dysfunction, and frustration. It's important to recognize that when we try to control people, it is out of fear. We try to prevent something that has not yet gone wrong from going wrong, and we are selfishly forcing our will onto another.

I am an optimist. I believe in the innate goodness of humanity. When tragedies occur, it seems our countrymen and women pull together in unity, even if it's for a short time. Consider the way our society rallied behind those in the Gulf Coast after Hurricane Katrina in 2005 or during the wildfires that swept through California and other parts of the west in 2017 and 2018. As a whole, we know how take care of each other. In times of trouble, epic disparity, and tragedy, we unite and solve problems together. Why does it take crises to bring this unity to the forefront? It doesn't have to. We, as leaders, have the responsibility to build safety and humanity back into the workplace. This is how we change the world.

In our professional worlds, we have the responsibility to push back if we don't agree with decisions. We can influence outcomes and provide suggestions, but there will be times when we may not be able to alter the executive level decisions that are made at our workplaces. This is particularly true if we work in a large company. If no changes are forthcoming, then we have a choice, and with choices come freedom. If we want to be good leaders, we must choose: fight, flee, or freeze, and we must choose bravely.

Choosing bravely–which ultimately leads to courage–is foundational for becoming a great leader. However, it's more complicated than simply making an intentional choice in the moment. I propose we are not born fearless. Rather, we are given conditions in life that position us to choose bravery over fear. Deep into his *Citizenship in a Republic* speech, Theodore Roosevelt made this statement: "...in the long run, success or failure will be conditioned upon the way in which the average man, the average woman, does his or her duty, first in the ordinary, every-day affairs of life, and next in those great occasional cries which call for heroic virtues." Bravery is one such heroic virtue. It's in those fear-filled moments when the leader within us can emerge victorious, if we so desire. The more instances we face and the more times we're able to think through and find our ability to be ourselves, the easier it becomes to choose ourselves again as we journey through life's various arenas.

I have been in those types of situations many times, the ones where I was faced with the choice to fight, flee, or freeze. In one particular season during my professional career, I was afraid to fail. I did not want to disappoint my leader. This fear of failure caused me to clamp down hard on the team I was leading, managing them from a place of fear. I overanalyzed my team's work. I had involved myself so deeply in the day-to-day tasks that I was directing work and assignments. I was basically undermining the authority of my leadership team. I inspected all the work and was overly critical of flaws but not generous with compliments. I had taken on the leadership style of my leader and lost myself in it. It nearly destroyed the team and myself. Much like a gladiatrix entering the arena to battle an enraged bear or lion while tens of thousands of spectators watched, I felt the pressure to perform, believing my success was an indicator of my worth. I can tell you from experience, it's not an effective way to lead in the workplace or in our personal lives. Anup Kochhar explains, "The fear of failure kills creativity and intelligence. The only thing it produces is conformity."

If one side of the leadership success coin is bravery, a flip of that coin will reveal its counterpart–authenticity. Before we dive into authenticity, I want us to know this truth: Perfection is an illusion. Another way to say this is that we are already perfect. We are all unique. If no one else in the world is exactly like us, we're perfect. So, if we are ourselves, just as we were made to be, we are perfect.

Authenticity is described as genuine, real, bona fide, true, and veritable. While these synonyms are accurate, I would add that authenticity requires us to be aware of what we are thinking and feeling (to know who we are) in specific moments of time. We are operating without authenticity if we are unaware of our current state of mind, not discerning our emotions, or if we are trying to be something we're not. Interestingly, we do not need to verbalize our internal truths in order to be authentic. There are many situations within a leader's day, week, and even life when simply knowing who he or she is may be the only factor required to be connected to oneself and maintain authenticity.

When people talk about authenticity, they sometimes refer to our *authentic selves*–which is a bit redundant in my opinion. Our actions and words are congruent with our beliefs and convictions. With the success of Brené Brown and others who have researched and fostered individual authenticity, it has become a widespread buzzword in recent years.

According to the Harvard Business Review, between 2008 and 2013 the number of articles mentioning the word "authenticity" per year has more than doubled. I don't believe all the hubbub will disappear any time soon, much like what happens with the latest fads. Authenticity is too essential–too foundational–for our very existence.

Ironically, our culture applauds authenticity while it simultaneously elevates inauthentic people. Social media is a prime example of this phenomenon. The world of social media allows people to regularly portray their best selves while hiding the parts of themselves they believe are not worthy of bearing. Social media marketing has been especially hit hard. At the writing of this book, Artificial Intelligence (AI) YouTubers are becoming increasingly popular. Facebook "friends" are not really friends. "Fans and followers" are not true fans and followers. In other words, they are not people who genuinely support brands or messages. Senior Editor, Lily Rothman, wrote in her *Time* article, "In the war for fans, authenticity was the first casualty, and the weapons deployed were sweepstakes, giveaways, contests and social game freebies." It seems we can't trust much of what we find online, yet we all seek out online platforms and information for connection.

Think of a moment when you have distanced yourself from your own inner truth– when your words did not align with your beliefs. For example, was there ever a time when you were frustrated with someone, but you decided to praise or validate that person for the very thing that bothered you? In order to support that person or approve his or her choice (a lie), you had to detach yourself from your own values and opinions. That detached feeling is indicative of inauthenticity, and it feels like crap. If repeated enough, we begin to lose our very selves and as leaders, we'll lose our credibility, influence, and perhaps even our teams.

While authenticity is necessary for great leadership, leaders themselves can easily misunderstand the concept. We often assume that authenticity is an innate quality—that a person is either authentic or not. In fact, authenticity is a quality that others must attribute to us. No leader can self-label. We are identified as authentic by what other people observe in us. It is for this reason that I propose we can learn how to be more authentic. If authenticity was simply an innate quality, there would be little we could do to manage it and, therefore, little we could do to make ourselves more effective as leaders.

While I have always found authenticity to be one of those elusive qualities that is difficult to live out consistently, I have likewise been told I am an authentic individual. I believe the reason for this is my ability to find contentment in expressing my rebellious self and not hiding my uniqueness. While most people strive for conformity in order to fit in, I learned how to strive for authenticity in order to be connected.

Fitting in is not the same as being connected. Fitting in requires us to become someone we are not in order to feel accepted. Being connected is when we are vulnerable and genuine, and we believe others accept us for who we truly are. We are all hard-wired with the desire for community, and we all have the emotional need to belong. It's not a weakness. I have found the most successful leaders are those who are the most connected. Those who are most connected with their team members are those who are the most authentic. The question then becomes *How do we create the environment where people feel safe enough to be vulnerable?* This is the paradox of vulnerability that I mentioned previously: Vulnerability feels weak to those who surrender to it and looks brave to those who experience it from someone else.

The reason for this is that authenticity positions us to connect with others on a more profound level. It allows others to see who we really are, shows people how we are going to behave, and gives us permission to make choices based on who we are. It opens doors for deeper conversations and open communication while eliminating the need for assumptions and masks. Much like wisdom is the practical use of knowledge and experience, authenticity is the practical application of transparency. The truth is what we know matters (and I'm sure we all know a lot), but who we are matters infinitely more. We can say we are excited or we can be genuinely excited through not only our words, but our thoughts, emotions, and choices. We can tell someone we understand their opinion, or we can show them the respect that true understanding provokes. We can emulate those around us, much like how chameleons change their colors, or we can live out our own convictions. We can pretend to be confident, or we can find our inner strengths and use them confidently.

Conforming to our true selves makes us trustworthy. Authentic leaders understand that everyone is perfect and have decided to cease striving for perfection. The drive for perfection is an illusion. We must love ourselves exactly as we are. When we do, we can feel fully satisfied in who we are, what we're doing, and how we relate to others. In fact, research over many years has proven that authenticity is directly proportional to our psychological health. David Williams wrote, "Authenticity has been linked to higher levels of positive affect, life satisfaction, autonomy, environmental mastery, positive relations with others, personal growth, self-acceptance, and reductions in stress and anxiety." Being true to oneself is not for the faint of heart, but it *will* satisfy one's heart.

Leadership demands the expression of an authentic self. So, how do we live and lead authentically? Williams also had this to offer (I took the liberty of changing the directives to make them "do's" rather than "don'ts" as Williams originally wrote):

- Act the way you feel.
- Remind yourself you can't please everyone.
- Focus on your own journey.
- Know your self-worth.
- Tell the truth.
- Be yourself.
- Learn from the past, focus on the present, and plan for the future.
- Make your own decisions.
- Own your mistakes and failures.
- Support others' success.
- Trust your gut feelings.
- Value experiences over things.
- Be kind.
- Have an open mind.
- Surround yourself with people who encourage you.

Much of this advice is relational in nature. Living authentically is not just about us. It's not simply about finding our comfort zones and striving for our own betterment. Authentic leadership is as much about supporting and connecting with those around us as it is about finding and expressing our true selves. Roz Usheroff reinforced this idea of support and connectivity when she wrote, "...authenticity is not based on only doing those things with which we are most comfortable or enjoy doing. Authenticity is remaining true to your motives or intent while working toward a *worthy and honorable goal*, that serves the best interests of others as well as your own."

Along these lines, I'd like to add a word of caution about our desire to be authentic. Finding and expressing your authentic self does not mean losing sight of the most basic of professional and personal skills that foster successful relationships. Whether we're in a workplace, family setting, or gathering of friends, there are key qualities we all want to present–flexibility, kindness, patience, self-control, and the ability to compromise to name a few. Chameleons successfully adjust to their surroundings but never cease being chameleons. Usheroff addressed this in her work when she wrote, "I see being a chameleon as someone who cares enough to adapt to others communication style, to read the temperature of a meeting, for example and change to be able to resolve issues, make people feel comfortable and so on. It doesn't necessarily mean changing who you are but being socially and/or politically savvy to understand that we need to be flexible."

The foundation for becoming an effective and trusted leader is to operate from both sides of the leadership coin. Leaders can be brave or authentic, but ideally we must learn how to effectively lead from these foundations simultaneously to construct deeper connections with the people around us. When we master both virtues, we uncover contentment in our role as a leaders and support high-performing teams over longer periods of time. In fact, it is not just contentment and team success that we find; we will also experience what it means to have a self-empowered life and true happiness.

~ 4 ~
BRAVERY GONE BAD

THE STORIES I share are ones I remember vividly, for the impacts they left on me were powerful. These are uncomfortable for me to tell, as they were not my best moments as a leader. In fact, they are stories of my failures as a leader. This book is about learning to be vulnerable as leaders in order to connect with those around us. My hope is that you can either relate to these stories based on your own experiences, or you can learn from them as you enter future arenas.

To understand these stories you need to understand from where my bravery came–or at least from where I think it came. As I've mentioned, I am the oldest of four siblings. I also have three step-siblings. Our family was wrought with dysfunction (as many families are). The dysfunction was not unique in any way, but my handling of the way it impacted me (my bravery) came from a deep-seeded fear of being hurt–not only emotionally, but also physically. This was not because my experience was filled with household violence; though, there were some of those moments, too. It was because as an infant who was frequently ill, I was subjected to a lot of pain and injury. Much of it was in the form of invasive procedures to save my life, but all that poking and prodding shaped how I perceived the world.

Therefore, one of my gremlins–or the recurring internal battles I fight–is my reflexive belief that people are dangerous and they will hurt me. To cope, my choices seemed to be to stay small, become invisible, or be scary. Oftentimes, I chose scary. Needless to say, being scary is not the best leadership philosophy.

These stories are meant to provide you with practical insights into how to create and maintain your own environments for developing success as a leader. They will be stories of my failures and later, my successes as a leader, told through the metaphor of the arena. As Roosevelt stated in his speech, "It is a mistake for any nation (or leader) to merely copy another; but it is even a greater mistake, it is a proof of weakness in any nation (or leader) not to be anxious to learn from one another and willing and able to adapt that learning to...make it fruitful and productive therein." I hope you can learn from my mistakes. In fact, I hope you already learned one critical lesson about failing through bravery from Chapter One. Here was the lesson:

When you choose your time to stand, be brave, respectful, and listen with an open mind.

I never recommend we keep quiet on issues of safety, security, laws, morals, and other obvious situations when we have a duty to act. The story of the rogue physician and my reaction in the Board of Directors meeting was an extreme example of bravery gone badly. What I *am* proposing is that leaders learn to be brave in the day-to-day moments; the subtler circumstances, when choices about how we respond are more difficult to make. Why? If we stay silent, it's these moments that can chip away at our resolve to be brave until suddenly someone acts in a way that violates our values or the values of the company, and we are either too afraid to speak up, or we don't even notice the violation anymore. That is not leadership at all.

> "Let not anyone pacify his conscience by the delusion that he can do no harm if he takes no part and forms no opinion. Bad men need nothing more to compass their ends than that good men should look on and do nothing."
> (British Philosopher, John Stuart Mill)

Many emotions resurfaced as I recalled this next story and lesson. I was new to a job in an Information Technology (IT) Department. I was walking down one of the hallways in the typical cubicle maze on my way to a large staff meeting, when a man stepped into the hallway. He held out his hand to welcome me to the team. It seemed innocent. However, it didn't stay that way. He proceeded to cross a physical boundary, and without getting into details here, I hauled off and clocked him.

Immediately, I went to my new leader and reported what had happened, fully aware that hitting him was not the best use of my choice to fight versus flee or freeze. My bravery did not think about the consequences of my response. Instead, it simply reacted to my need for protection. While there were many repercussions after that incident, none of them included an investigation by the Human Resources (HR) Department. No one seemed to care about why I did what I did in that moment. The outcome of my bravery explosion was that I was suspended without pay for a week. [Suddenly, I feel pissed off just writing out this story.] I was wrong when I reacted to his behavior with physical retaliation, but he was wrongER. I'll share more later about this, but for now, the lesson is important to share:

> **When you are wronged in a way that violates your values, safety, or security, get help (and to safety) before you react or choose to fight in a professional setting. Do not be shy; use your voice. Do not brush it off. Act; don't react.**

The next example I am about to share could be titled "Some Things Never Change." At the time when this story unfolded, I had been on my leadership journey for quite some time–decades, actually. I had a number of successes and some failures along the way. I was proud of where I was and what I was doing. The people with whom I was working were great; they were smart, thoughtful, and engaging. I often thought, *What could be better?* I felt like I was part of a high-performing team, at both the peer and leadership levels. However, long-standing habits are hard to break. Suddenly, everything seemed to change–as it usually does–and I found myself in a completely different arena.

There was one person who entered the arena and became the center of my disquiet. I could not put my finger on what it was about him that made my skin crawl, but I am certain everyone has met someone like that. You know what I am attempting to describe. In this case, I could not choose to walk away and avoid him. He was a peer with whom I had to work on a regular basis. To say I was struggling would be an understatement. The techniques he used to manipulate people were nothing short of artistry, and he continued to avoid accountability, even when he was disengaged or failed to deliver.

Now as a female leader, there were times when female employees from other groups came to me to get help with issues or challenges they were having with their own leaders. Frequently, one of those who sought my advice was this particular leader's administrative assistant. The relationship between a leader and his or her administrative assistant is a sacred one and not easily recovered if trust is betrayed. For this employee to reach out to me, I knew it must be bad. I won't get into her stories, but they were validations of my opinion about this leader's lack of character. The purpose of this information is to show you the history behind my responses and choices in the face of someone else's actions.

I felt belittled by his words; he criticized my work and attempted to control me as some sort of power grab. I am not sure how to explain it, but what I felt was akin to being bullied. By now you know that when I feel threatened, in comes Scary Mary. I became especially scary because the other choices I used to cope–being small or invisible–are exactly what most bullies want from their targets. I refused to give him that satisfaction.

When we think of bullies, we likely think of schoolyards or bus stops. That's exactly like what our work environment became. We tussled and fought just like kids on the playground. We took turns throwing the proverbial sand in the sandbox, not playing well with each other at all.

One specific example that may paint the best picture of bravery gone badly is a phone call I had with this individual. The situation was, from my point of view, very straightforward. My leader had called me and asked me to work with him to transition specific employees from his team to my team. The decision had already been made, and all that was left was the paperwork and communication. So, I made the call.

"Hey! How are you? I just got a call from [my leader] letting me know about the meeting you just had. I am looking to put a plan together for the transition of your staff members to my team."

He replied, "Well, we need to talk about that. I am not sure we got to a final, *final* decision."

"I am confused. It seemed pretty clear from [my leader] that it was final. So we need to move forward with a plan," I patiently said.

"Not really. We need to talk about it." He persisted.

"I am not sure what we need to talk about. I wasn't at the meeting, so perhaps you need to go back to those who were there and make sure you're clear because [my leader] was very clear with me."

"Look...First, I think they would be disappointed if we can't figure this out ourselves. They rely on us to be leaders. Second, I can have a conversation with [your leader] whenever I want to, so I am not sure what the issue is." It seemed he wasn't going to let this go, and with that last statement, I felt he had threatened me. So, I put on my warrior boots.

"Well, I don't give a crap who you talk to, and I am not going to negotiate something with you that has already been decided. In my view, we have two choices: Move forward with a plan or you go back to the group and get clarity on what is supposed to happen."

This went on, back and forth for a bit, until I decided it was escalating past the point of no return and tried to bring it back to some civil discourse. This is the response I received from him:

"Well, you started this, so now this is how it's going to go..."

I cut him off. "Fine! Bring it! Let's go..."

Needless to say, neither the first words nor the rest of my outburst were constructive, relationship-enhancing, or beneficial. So, what is the takeaway?

Bullies are everywhere. They don't just disappear when we leave school. In fact, the business arena is a place where they can thrive, especially when they believe they've been given some power. This lesson:

Never rise to the bait of bullies. In reality, it knocks you down to their level.

In this next story, I was working in a role that someone else had requested I take. The relationships between those involved were filled with distrust, and I found myself in conflict with one of my colleagues. She was a younger woman, and I worked hard to build rapport while we labored to build a case for my leader.

The day I presented the case, she was outwardly supportive. However two days later, she betrayed my trust and confided in my leader that she did not believe in my work or in me. I was already in a state of heightened awareness since my leader at the time was wildly unpredictable. In fact, my private moniker for her was "tornado in a teacup." I never knew what she was going to do. She was rarely consistent with her thoughts or actions. When my coworker went behind my back, it became a situation that demanded I choose to fight or flee.

I called my colleague and informed her–in my typical straightforward approach–that I could no longer trust her. Her actions had effectively destroyed her integrity. Unsurprisingly, my words caused her to become defensive. I shut down the conversation by saying, "If you don't have what it takes to sit at the big kids' table, perhaps you should go home."

Obviously, this was not a helpful way to pair bravery with authenticity. I agree with Roosevelt's list of the qualities found in "masterful people." Some of those characteristics are self-mastery, common sense, courage, and the power of accepting individual responsibility, yet acting in conjunction with others. At this time in my life, I had not quite mastered the ability to portray my authentic self with courage or tact.

I found myself forced to sit in a cesspool of danger. I felt threatened from every direction: her leader, my leader, and naturally, from this woman. I was invited–no, summoned is a better word–to the corporate office to have a conversation about the incident. There were no pre-meeting questions from my leader, no curiosity about my perspective of the situation, and no attempt to seek understanding. The tension in the workplace had just become palpable.

I sat in my office preparing for the meeting when my leader knocked on my door. "We're not going to approve your requisition to hire more staff." It was the only thing she mentioned. There was no reference to the upcoming meeting upstairs.

"That's great. Then I just need to know what I should stop doing."

She simply walked away. I continued to prepare. A few minutes later, I received an IM (instant message) from her. I thought with annoyance, *Your office is steps away from mine and you were just here!* I went to see what she wanted.

"I hope you're ready for this meeting because it's going to be bad. It's going to be really bad."

I stared at her for a few moments, and then I found my voice. "I'm ready for the meeting, and honestly, if you don't have my back, you'll have my badge." I pivoted and walked out of her office.

It was a turning point in my career. In those seconds, I chose bravery that stemmed from a deep courage that had been carefully groomed. I chose my own authentic response to a situation I felt I had no control over. I communicated my needs. In those few ticks of the clock, I decided to stand up for my values, my work, and myself. I chose to fight (or flee, if warranted), risking my job for what I believed in and not melting in the face of the threat. Make no mistake–it was not that I was fearless; my heart rate was elevated, and my skin was likely flushed. Yet, I chose to be brave in order to be honest.

The meeting itself was preposterous. Four women sat around a table. There was my leader, my colleague, her leader, and me. Despite the outright warning from my leader, we discussed nothing related to the conflict and nothing about the hiring freeze. I am not kidding. When it seemed the meeting had come to a close, I spoke up.

"Was that the meeting?"

They confirmed the meeting was over and never alluded to the original purpose for it. I knew at that moment that I would never understand nor be able to control what my colleague or those leaders were going to do. In the next moment, I made the intentional decision to stop stressing about all of it. Here is what I learned:

Stand up for what you believe in. Once you lose your integrity, it's not easily won back. The universe will take care of the rest, or as my grandfather used to say, "What goes around, comes around."

It wasn't long after this incident that the universe brought in new leadership and my world changed. My new leader and I were able to form a relationship built on respect.

Now, I am not surmising that every brave moment will happen (or should happen) like this. In fact, no one should have to encounter tornadoes in teacups like the one I shared about in this story. Most times, we will not have the flexibility or resources to say we can walk away from a job. It's not often a viable solution, and we should not make empty threats. What I am encouraging us to do is realize our journeys are defined by how we respond to those things that pop up from the depths, like those wild animals on the pulleys in ancient Rome. We must be prepared to make choices when we're confronted with challenges and fear. How we choose will depend on the significance of the challenge. A strong, hungry lion is different than a battle-weary ostrich. As Martin Luther King, Jr. wrote, "The ultimate measure of a person is not where he or she stands in moments of comfort or convenience, but where he or she stands at times of challenge and controversy."

The reality is that given the definitions of bravery I shared in the previous chapter, my first experiences in carrying out my bravery did not go so well. I was impulsive, passionate, and blind when being brave. As you can image, in the world of business, this is not considered respectable. I performed well and had results, but I frequently left broken relationships in my wake. I regularly received feedback saying I was not cognizant of others' feelings. While I didn't like it, I wasn't sure what to do about it because it was never followed up with coaching for improvement. I continued to struggle and fall down, get back up, and find myself in the same fight again, wondering why the outcome wasn't any different.

It would take learning more about myself to make the necessary changes.

~ 5 ~
ABSENT AUTHENTICITY

BEFORE WE MOVE into the practical strategies for leading with authentic bravery, I believe it's critical to wrap a few stories around the foundation of authenticity. Before we can ever succeed in the public arenas of life (such as the arena of leadership), we must first gain victory over the private battles within ourselves. I learned this lesson the hard way–over multiple moments when my authenticity was absent.

If our authentic selves can be missing or hidden, how can we know for certain when we are being authentic? Do we just know? Or is it much more subtle than that?

When we lose our authentic selves, I believe we know it immediately, and in a profoundly deep place. Some people have described a gut, or core level, response that signals their discontent. Others hear a soft, internal voice that whispers warnings about straying from self. Regardless of how your body responds or your self-talk sounds, there are red flags when we are not living out our true selves–when our internal thoughts, feelings, and wills are not aligned with our external words, behaviors, and attitudes. There are also consequences.

"You are so authentic." I have heard this statement countless times. I am not sure if it is as true as people believe it to be. While my bravery was evident from day one of my professional career, it was not until the end of my corporate journey that my authentic self showed up consistently. Sometimes, I think others saw my bravery and mistook it for the whole of my authentic self. It's true that bravery is a visible piece of who I am. Here's the thing, though: My authentic self is so much more than just my bravery.

I believe leaders are more successful at building relationships and teams when we focus on individual strengths rather than weaknesses. One cannot achieve excellence by mitigating weakness. If we utilize everyone's strengths, we become a formidable unit, each person adding his or her best selves to the team or project. I spent quite some time uncovering and unlocking all my strengths (not just my bravery) and now help others do the same. I have relied heavily on Tom Rath's book, *StrengthsFinder 2.0* (and the corresponding assessments) while coaching leaders through professional and personal development.

According to this assessment, my top five talents or strengths are strategic, relator, restorative, intellection, and command. You would need to source the book to know the definitions of these labels, but for the most part they tell a story. The story is of an individual (me) who is able to

- Create alternative ways to proceed when faced with challenges.
- Easily see patterns and find solutions.
- Appreciate and engage in introspective thoughts and discussions.
- Find deep satisfaction in working with others toward a shared goal.
- Take control of a situation while making decisions quickly.

I like to think this mosaic of strengths served me well on my leadership journey and continues to do so in my coaching practice.

Recently, I was introduced to the VIA Character Strengths and Virtues, another assessment tool which identifies talents and positive attributes. The top five strengths that surfaced during this test were bravery (duh!), judgment, perseverance, love, and honesty. These were very closely followed by creativity, fairness, perspective, teamwork, and humor.

So, why am I telling you all this? Well initially, only two of these attributes showed up regularly in my work life: bravery and command. And it took quite some time for me to express those two strengths *well*. In the earliest years of my career, I chose not to say what I wanted to say, I did not ask for clarity when I needed it, and I decided to stay in whatever false story I was telling myself about a specific situation instead of engaging with others and having a voice. This inauthenticity made me hyper-vigilant, always ready for the next confrontation. I was operating with only a portion of my true self. The parts of me that I kept hidden were my very strengths: perspective, love, and being able to relate to others and restore relationships. So, while others showered me with affirmation about my authenticity, in truth, I felt half empty.

When the whole of our authentic selves isn't showing up, it is draining. Suddenly, we become discontent with where we are, what we're doing, and even who we are. Ultimately, our very purpose can spiral down that drain and out of sight. Here's the thing–when that happens, we start carrying around a lot of crap. If we keep it up, we eventually turn that fairy tale of what we can and cannot do into the reality. We begin to believe our discontent, and the emptiness feels like all we are. We'll need a concierge service to manage all that baggage.

We can't get rid of one hundred percent of our baggage (trust me, I've tried), as some of it remains to keep us humble, honest, and always learning. However, we can try to keep it to the size of an overnight bag. The only way to do that is to show up in front of others and unpack all of ourselves.

Look, I am not saying that all the crap in our luggage has to be on public display–especially at work–but I am saying we have to unpack our strengths, personalities, and talents so we can be our best selves. We have to be able to show up, engage, and lead. It is that simple, and it is that hard. Believe me; it's hard. It is scary to be vulnerable, and this time, I'm not referring to Scary Mary. It is one of those things that requires a tablespoon of faith to accomplish. You just have to unpack the bag and trust that the contents are worthy, because they are. No one can do it for you. The contents are too valuable.

> "When you get to the end of all the light you know and it's time to step into the darkness of the unknown, faith is knowing that one of two things shall happen: either you will be given something solid to stand on, or you will be taught how to fly." (Edward Teller, Theoretical Physicist)

I have walked through many stories about how I failed to show up and be authentic, despite all the affirmation that I was an authentic person. One story involved that previous bully and me. As I mentioned, this individual was an arrogant and manipulative person. His biggest weapons were passive aggressiveness and shaming others, and I fell for the bait. I believed his goal was to make me look bad. I felt disrespected, as if he never considered my ideas or my feelings at all. In this particular case, he hit me with every lie I was trying hard not to believe about myself. Every time I came in contact with him, it brought me to my knees (figuratively). This caused me to feel angry, threatened, and small. My anger didn't actually manifest itself outwardly. It was more of a quiet anger–a blinding, red, seething anger–that bubbled under the surface. I wanted to either scream or cry...or both. I tried to win his approval on countless occasions, but it never worked. I now know one cannot win approval from these types of people through effort or achievement.

In reaction to his behavior, I failed to show up. I did not use my voice; I was not being authentic. Instead, I engaged in gossip, played the blame-game, and sought validation from others. Look, we all have our moments where we become our own form of a critic in the face of our harshest critics. This was one of those times for me.

Several teams had been assigned the task of developing strategies for the products in our business (building a business case, mining market data, etc.) I was having a difficult time getting everyone together to get the work done. So, I decided to treat it like a wedding. Everyone was invited, but if you chose not to come, we were still going to get married. I reserved a conference room for the day, sent the invitation, and went to work. This particular individual chose not to participate but sent some of his team members instead. That was good. At least he had representation.

We were hard at work in the conference room on the "wedding day" and making good progress when he unexpectedly showed up. He had a big personality, and he began to take over the meeting, which was still fine with me. I was happy to have the help and his participation. At several points during the meeting, I disagreed with his ideas and made alternate suggestions. I am not sure how much time had passed, but suddenly, he asked me to step out in the hall. Goodbye nice wedding.

The first trigger for me was the fact he asked me to step out in the hall *in front of his staff*. Then, he proceeded to give me a lecture on leadership in the f*cking hallway. (Yes, it still makes me mad when I think about it.) At this point, I had been a leader for over twenty years, and I was a good one. What added to my anger was that the content of his lecture was dead wrong, which isn't important for this story. The point is, I did nothing. I said nothing. I just stared at him, and when he was done, I walked back into the room and never said another word. So, his bullying worked.

The second time we collided was when I called him to let him know that the person he had assigned to a project I was leading was not getting the work done. He asked if I had talked to the person. (That's Leadership 101–of course I had!) I confirmed I had spoken with his staff member already and that no improvements had been made, so I requested a different person to help me. Instead, he gathered the three of us on the phone together and preceeded to council the two of us as if I f*cking worked for him. Again, I was red hot. So, what did I do? Nothing. Well, I did call my leader to complain about it, which I don't recommend doing. However, I never dealt with it directly. I was not interacting authentically with this individual. I carried the anger and his mistreatment of me around in my luggage, adding more weight with each passing encounter. It was not until years later that I was able to unpack it and understand that it was likely this peer of mine who was the insecure one. Perhaps he even thought he was being helpful. Why did he trigger me so badly? His words and choices pushed all my negative self-talk buttons, the ones labeled "not good enough" and "imposter." I lived as if someone was going to figure out that I was the one who wasn't supposed to be sitting at the big kids' table. When the truth was, I was a good leader.

"If someone is mistreating you, make sure you aren't treating yourself in the same manner." (Kim Honeycutt, Psychotherapist and Author)

A quick note about internal triggers—we all have them. I will dive deeper into them in a future chapter, but for now know this: They are internal switches that can be triggered when certain things occur, specific smells or sounds are experienced, or certain words are uttered. They come from a place of love but they don't feel like they do. Gremlins show up in order to protect us from something that happened when we were young, not realizing the time and place of the painful memory are long gone. The thoughts and subsequent feelings they produce are not valid. As adults, we have to learn to manage them in order to be able to find and live out our authentic selves. In terms of the arena of self, they are some of our inner critics.

Everyone has insecurities. Don't let yours get triggered by someone else's. Your negative talk is not who you are, and you should not let it define you.

The next story is about one of the more difficult leaders I had along the way. Honestly, that description is an understatement. No matter what I did, she was not pleased. Nothing seemed to be good enough. Nothing I accomplished met her lofty expectations. She was always on me about something. I was good at my job, and I worked really hard. There was no reason for this type of treatment. Again, I learned much later down the road that it was not really about me. However, at the time I didn't know that.

Remember, thoughts lead to feelings, which in turn, lead to behaviors (or put another way, how you show up). I thought she believed I was really bad at my job and feared she was going to fire me at any moment. I felt unworthy and that somehow I was a failure, so I showed up as disengaged, reactive, and at times, absent. What made this worse was that I projected all this junk in my bag onto those around me. I became an overpowering, micromanaging leader. It sucked for everyone!

I complained to anyone who would listen, but I never addressed my frustration with my leader. I learned to hate my job, which up to this point, I had loved. I had felt like a rock star. Then, I became the critical fan, high up in the stands. My attitude became angry and defensive as I avoided addressing these thoughts and emotions. Basically, I neglected myself and judged everyone around me. I never asked for what I really needed. How did this resolve itself? Well… that is another story for another time, but the point is that I never made it right, and it took a long time for me to find my voice again. The lesson to grab here:

If you find yourself in the cheap seats, find your way back to the arena. If you're lost, get help.

Our saving grace is when we finally decide to stop and respond authentically–not hide or react poorly–to those who are difficult. When we respond with our voices and our full set of strengths, they bring us back to ourselves. I now understand that much of others' poor behaviors were not about me; however at the time, I absolutely thought they were. I was personalizing their mistreatment of me. We all do that at times, don't we? We must remember that our thoughts impact our feelings, which in turn, affect our behavior. We get to choose if our thoughts and subsequent behaviors will be positive or negative. It's our choice to unpack our bags and live without the burdens of our gremlins.

As we rise from the darkness of fear and emerge vulnerably into the light, we are experiencing special and short-lived moments when we are forced to choose how we are going to live. With the foundations of bravery and authenticity, we can choose wisely. We can be leaders that journey through our various arenas, full of the knowledge that we are being who we are meant to be. We can ask for the things we need and speak up for those things no one else is brave enough to mention. As Brené Brown expertly wrote in *Daring Greatly*, "Courage starts with showing up and letting ourselves be seen." Or, we can be leaders who try to be something we are not, living outside ourselves, continuously trying to prove our own worthiness, battling with our true selves forever, and lead from a place of fear. The choice is ours to make as we ascend from the "basement."

If we choose bravery and authenticity, we will connect with the people around us, including team members, colleagues, friends, and family members. This connection provides those around us with a sense of belonging. And, when people feel they belong because of our intentional acts of bravery and authenticity, they will follow us.

~ 6 ~
FORGING WEAPON #1:
SELF-MASTERY

THE ANCIENT GLADIATORS' weapons were their tools of the trade. If you were to put a gladius sword or pugio (dagger) into the hands of a well-trained gladiator, you would instantly have an expert–a fighting machine capable of ending a life in seconds. Every time a gladiator or gladiatrix stepped into the amphitheater, they put their trust in their weapons. Interestingly, each class or level of gladiator in ancient Rome had his or her own unique weapon or set of weapons.

To develop a meaningful level of comfort, show leadership proficiency, establish stability and peace, and ultimately become successful at leading high-performing teams, we must hone the skills necessary to stand in the leadership arena. Forging leadership-specific weapons prepares us for increasing responsibilities and further advancement. The first tool we will look at is self-mastery. It's the most important weapon leaders must master, and the one from which the other three tools are forged.

In the center of the arena, we find our warrior. In order to find victory, the warrior must discover and appreciate her strengths. She must bring forth and utilize her fierceness, competitive nature, and the weapons in her possession. She must be cognizant of the blind spots in the arena, the areas she cannot see where foes lurk just before their attack. The warrior must acknowledge her old wounds, the ones that left scars–physical, mental, and emotional–so that she can recognize the triggers that might unleash fear. She'll want to keep those fears in check during the struggle. The warrior must also enlist ways to maintain her motivation to battle and ultimately win. Without a driving desire to survive, the beast on the opposite end of the arena will defeat her. Finally, entertaining an optimistic attitude gives her confidence to succeed. In all of these ways, it's apparent that self-discovery and self-control are the keys to victory in the arena. They are the same key factors we leaders need to be successful across our lives.

In simple terms, self-mastery is knowing ourselves well enough to regulate ourselves. It is the by-product of self-discovery and self-control. It's recognizing, understanding, and owning the whole of our strengths, blind spots, struggles, motivations, triggers, and attitude. In his speech, Theodore Roosevelt directly addressed self-mastery as a key component to becoming someone of influence:

> "Self-restraint, self-mastery, common sense, the power of accepting individual responsibility and yet of acting in conjunction with others, courage and resolution–these are the qualities which mark a masterful people."

SELF-DISCOVERY

First, we dive into the story of self. The core of who we are encompasses three distinct areas: our thoughts and beliefs, our feelings or emotions, and our actions. Our behaviors are the total output of these three core components. There is a clear process that governs every one of our actions. What happens in our minds–in essence the content of our thoughts and beliefs–drives our emotions, and our emotions tend to influence our actions and behaviors. This can be both a blessing and a curse, depending on that content.

When the stories we tell ourselves or the information others tell us (the content of what we think, hear, read, believe, and see) are encouraging and true, our feelings will be more positive, productive, and purposed. Great leaders know how to rely on and trust constructive inputs in order to produce outputs ripe for leading.

When our beliefs and thoughts are based on lies, false assumptions, and past hurts, negative emotions follow suit. Feelings of inadequacy, loneliness, and fear can fuel our behavior, and when that happens, our behavior is not indicative of our best selves. As we strive for self-mastery, we learn to see the negative content for what it is. We understand the tall tales that exist in our heads, diminish the amount of false information we believe, and halt the process at the point our emotions affect our choices.

Leaders must understand more than just thoughts and emotions. We must also know our strengths. Dr. Tal Ben-Shahar, a doctor of psychology and Harvard lecturer, teaches we possess two basic categories of strengths. The first is passion-based strengths, and the second is performance-based (skills) strengths. We find ourselves operating "in the zone," as athletes might say, when we reach the crossroads of our passions and our skills. It's the place where what we love and what we excel at intersect.

For example, I am skilled at analyzing numbers. This performance strength allowed me to excel in my operations and accounting roles, but I never had a passion for number crunching alone. It wasn't until my responsibilities expanded and I started to solve complex problems and develop strategies for improvement that my passion was ignited around number analysis and operations.

As a side note, I've never liked the term "problem-solver." I always thought it had a negative connotation. So, I coined the word "solutionist" to describe my superpower ability to identify solutions to problems. Take a moment now to think about the strengths you offer as a leader. Now, let's discuss passions.

My personal passions are leadership, honesty, and love. They happen to revolve around relationships. I'm at my best when I'm helping and coaching others to know truth and be the best versions of themselves. Do you know what your passions are?

Leadership blind spots are the specific areas where a leader–even a very successful leader–is missing something. It is an oversight in a specific area, character flaw, or a part of our skillset that was never adequately developed. "Blind spots can be the Achilles heel of leadership. Weaknesses are aspects that we can intentionally strengthen with practice, time, or desire. Blind spots, however, are personal traits or aspects we don't even know about that may limit the way we act, react, behave or believe, and therefore limit our effectiveness." These blind spots can sabotage even the most promising leaders if they are left undiscovered.

There are dozens of potential blind spots. Examples include the disregard of our instincts, our tendency to avoid difficult conversations, failure to ask for help, decision-making based on biases, distrust of the wisdom or expertise of our team members, or the failure to learn from past patterns or lessons while consistently blaming others.

One of the most effective ways to discover our blind spots is to ask the people closest to us. Again, the definition of a blind spot is an area of deficiency we don't even know is there. In the business world, blind spots can be revealed through various assessments.

While not a hell of a lot of fun, these assessments are imperative to understanding not only our blind spots but also how we show up as leaders. They are typically broken down into four major groupings–identity, reputation, values, and attitude. There are options for more narrow focus areas, such as communication styles, as well.

Self-discovery is just the first half of self-mastery. Leaders who learn about but choose to ignore their strengths and passions or continue to miss their blind spots are susceptible to emotional triggers and will face serious challenges when they are promoted into more senior-level roles. Therefore, it's important to master the second half of self-mastery, as well–self-control.

Self-Control

Self-control is the ability to use what we know about ourselves so we can manage all of the internal and external triggers that come our way. It is the quality we refine that will allow us to stop ourselves from doing things we might want to do but that may not be in our best interests. For leaders at any level, this is crucial, and the stakes get higher the further up any leadership chain we move.

Self-control is important in relation to our strengths and passions because when taken too far, strengths can become our biggest weaknesses. One of my strengths is bravery. As you've read in a previous chapter, "Bravery Gone Bad," I had to learn self-control in order to harness my bravery and not let it control me through impulsive words and actions.

Self-control is not easy. Knee-jerk reactions happen. Sometimes, they are unconscious responses that come from blind spots we have that are triggered by certain events, words, or people. The good news is that we can "unact" if needed. We can apologize, chase down our impulsive reactions, explain ourselves, be vulnerable, and (if all that freaks you out right now), at least learn to pause, breath, and regroup.

I'm referring to our ability to use feeling words to help explain a behavior. A simple response such as, "When I heard [abc], I felt [xyz]" can repair many relationships that are left in tension after our lack of self-control. We all have the opportunity to step into that moment and correct it as soon as possible. We also have the opportunity to apologize for our *behavior*, rather than defend our thoughts or feelings, which are always valid. When we do this, trust and respect can be re-built almost instantaneously.

Many of us have heard about the importance of emotional intelligence (measured in terms of an emotional quotient or EQ and similar to IQ) in leadership. The term was introduced into mainstream culture in 1995 when Daniel Goleman, a psychologist and journalist, took the work of psychologists John Mayer and Peter Salovey regarding emotions and argued that our standard intellectual appraisals must be expanded to include EQ. It takes a special kind of intelligence, Goleman said, to process emotional information and utilize it effectively–whether to facilitate good personal decisions, resolve conflict, or motivate others.

One of the pitfalls of a lower EQ is succumbing to our emotional triggers. Triggers are the kinds of things in our environment that hit a deeply rooted pain or trauma from our past. This results in an influx of emotions. External triggers are words, behaviors, or types of people that activate our fight, flee, or freeze responses, not necessarily because of what the other person has said or done, but because what they said or did reminded our subconscious of a past hurt.

Sometimes the response we have when triggered (often called our stress response, or how we respond under pressure or when we are not self monitoring) is appropriate. Sometimes it isn't. That response can inhibit the work we want to accomplish. Worse yet, when fight or flee responses are fully engaged, we may treat those around us like enemies rather than colleagues. In essence, triggers derail us from becoming the kind of leader, coworker, parent, or spouse we want to be. Recognizing and managing our triggers is one of the first steps toward self-awareness and self-control; it is vital to a leader's success.

One of my own triggers is when I feel there is a lack of respect coming from a peer. Respect is one of my top emotional needs. It says I'm valued. If someone says or does something that pushes that personal hot button, there is a flood of emotions. The thought, or story, I tell myself is that I must not be good enough. The feelings attached to that mindset include anger and frustration. Both stem from fear, a deep-rooted belief that perhaps the truth is that I am, in fact, not good enough. I don't belong at the big kids' table, so to speak.

An example of a time this trigger was pressed was when I believed a peer was intentionally trying to make me look bad. I thought he was compiling the evidence of my mistakes, and I frequently danced between attack and defense mode during our interactions. During an attack mode episode, I became much like the warrior in the middle of a battle. I moved forward aggressively and confronted my peer one day in a group setting. In this particular moment, I was operating with my swirling emotions, and I was not delivering the message I wanted to convey with any kind of tact.

After the initial clash, we stepped into the hallway and out of the group setting. I was bubbling up with anger–the root cause being my long-standing fears of rejection and of failing. Anger is so much easier to feel than fear because it gives us a (false) sense of power. I was on the verge of tears. Crying is a big fat no-no in corporate America, especially for women. Staring at the ground to hide my dampening eyes, I managed to say, "Just don't listen to me right now; I have old records playing, and this has nothing to do with you. I just need a moment." Then, I walked away.

I was mad at myself...and quite embarrassed. Yet, I was also proud of myself because I had used my voice to shut down the opportunity for that peer to hold onto a negative impression of me. I was proud of my ability to be authentic and brave in the middle of an emotional tailspin. The fact I was able to recognize my triggers, understand how they were affecting my emotions, and find a small measure of vulnerable humility in that moment, made a powerful and lasting difference in my relationship with that peer moving forward.

This might be the hardest part of being a leader–the humility that is required for self-mastery. It's a tall order. We're human. When we've had a lapse in self-control, we can–no, we should–backtrack and partner with humility to help those on the receiving end of our outbursts feel more connected and respected. The less we can leave people feeling bruised after our encounters with them, the better the leader we will become. I've often used this quote from Maya Angelou in my coaching sessions: "I've learned that people will forget what you said, people will forget what you did, but people will never forget how you made them feel."

This entire equation (self-discovery + self-control = self-mastery) is wrapped up in our attitudes. Our energy, outlook, and the amount of confidence in our success impact our ability to lead others and ourselves.

How we untangle negative attitudes and bring optimism into our arenas will be a determining factor in the level of success we achieve.

Attitudes can do one of two things: They either build up or tear down. Our attitudes affect our actions in more ways than one, because they impact those around us as well. A wonderful truth is that we get to choose our attitudes. They do not have to be married to our circumstances. We can opt for an open attitude and change the outcome of both our actions and our environment.

As you can see, there are numerous derailers–as I like to call them–to our success as a leader. Derailment occurs with our inability to react well to stressors. I'm not referring to working under stress. Some measure of stress can be a productive motivator. However, stressors overwhelm us, violate our values, and become career derailers. Failing to master one's self is a major stressor. It's why this weapon of successful leadership is so critical to sharpen. I would be remiss as a leader and coach if I did not share some of the symptoms of workplace derailers to watch out for and a few strategies for how to master self in pursuit of your leadership roles:

Symptoms

- If you are working hard and getting decent results, but you are missing out on big projects or promotions, take some time to figure out what derailer is affecting your career progression.
- If you are the leader of a team or group, and you frequently end up doing most of the work, there may be a blind spot to uncover.
- If you go to a conference with a group and during the breaks or lunch, you are not included in the social gatherings, there may be an underlying issue to unravel.

- If you present a new idea or facilitate a presentation and get no feedback or questions, there may be a derailer at work in your arena.

- If you are constantly feeling worried or anxious, you may need to adjust your outlook (attitude) regarding your circumstances. Remember it's a choice to view a situation as an opportunity rather than a barrier.

STRATEGIES

- Self-discovery begins by surrounding yourself with friends and family who will tell it like it is. A friend calls this her personal board of directors. You don't want validation from these individuals. You want honesty.

- If you do not feel like you are utilizing your strengths in your role, figure out where the gaps are and make any possible changes to your environment or tasks in order to move toward your passions and skill set. Sometimes, you may have to adjust your calendar to live out your passions elsewhere for a period of time.

- Avoid spending too many resources (time, energy, funding) on developing weaknesses in the hopes they become strengths. Use your resources to support you and your team's strengths and passions.

- Invest in the time and resources needed to get a clear picture of yourself so you can determine how you show up and what you want to address.

- Understand your values. Our values and leadership derailers are intertwined. When we know what we stand for, it becomes a point of clarity–for others as well as ourselves. Build your decisions around your values.

- Check your attitude regarding the challenges you face. Attitudes are contagious. The proverbial cup-half-full perspective can affect your behavior and the attitudes of those around you in a profound way.

- Surround yourself with a team of people with diverse viewpoints who are not afraid to engage in "productive debates" in order to move the team toward its collective goals.

Speaking of "debates" or fights, there is one battle toward the victory of self-mastery that requires some extra training to overcome its potent influence on our leadership success. In every arena, there are critics. There are those who will look for our faults, weaknesses, and emotional hot buttons. They will exploit them, so it's imperative we know whom (or what) they are and how to fight back. There is one category of critics that relate directly to self-mastery. They are called our inner critics, and we're about to discover out how to identify and dismantle them.

~ 7 ~
FIGHTING THE INNER CRITIC

ONE OF THE key battles involved in mastering self is the ability to recognize and deal with our critics. As you may recall from our metaphor of the arena, the critics are the naysayers up in the stands. A critic is a package of preconceptions wrapped carelessly in fear. They judge our choices, words, and certainly our faults.

While most critics sit furthest from the action, there is one type of critic for which this is not true. Our inner critics are extremely close to us–deep down inside. If we are going to talk about self-mastery, we must include a discussion about inner critics. Who are they? Actually, it's more like *what* are they? Inner critics are our own negative thoughts, critical self-talk, limiting beliefs, assumptions, interpretations, and emotional buttons that have been shaped by our past experiences–sometimes even by trauma.

LIMITING BELIEFS

First, let's talk about our thoughts. Everyone has thoughts, and they can be positive, negative, or neutral. The thinking process organizes information in order to give it meaning and promote function. Inside a child's brain, information first manifests as data through our five senses. Then, our thinking (both subconscious and conscious) begins to organize this data as we mature. In a nutshell, every thought is directly related to information gathered through the senses and is influenced by our attitudes, personality, education, environment, and past experiences.

If our childhoods are fraught with stress, adverse experiences, fear, or any other negative encounter, our thoughts are adversely affected as well. We begin to believe things about the world that aren't true. These are called limiting beliefs. Limiting beliefs are the lies we learn about how to think about certain circumstances and life itself. Some of our cultural expressions can be misunderstood, contributing to our limiting beliefs as well. An example of a limiting belief I used to struggle with was the idea *to forgive is to forget*. I thought that if I forgave someone, it meant I wasn't allowed to feel the pain of the injustice anymore.

I conducted an informal survey. I cannot say it was statistically relevant, but it was meaningful. I asked the people with whom I was in conversation, "What does the word *try* mean to you?" I was amazed that most of them (close to 80%) equated the word *try* with failure. Many of them quoted Yoda, the Jedi Master from Star Wars. "Do. Or do not. There is no try."

Then, I conducted some online searches using the words try and fail. The headline results read:

- This Phrase Instantly Destroys Your Credibility–"I will try."
- Trying is Failing
- The Difference Between Trying and Doing

I also found these headlines:

- If you don't try, you've already failed.
- If you're not failing, you're probably not trying as hard as you could be.

I found this somewhat polarizing point of view interesting. I believe most of these philosophies have done us a disservice. They've shifted our mindsets and attitudes about doing something new to make it seem negative or scary. The majority of us may very well believe that trying is fundamentally bad because our limiting beliefs have made it the opposite of succeeding.

Here is what I believe is important to us as leaders: Change is a journey worth taking, and the first step toward change is a willingness to try. I believe Yoda was talking about mindset and belief, not action. After all, it took Luke several attempts to get that ship out of the swamp. So, I agree with Yoda in that regard. I also agree with famed automaker Henry Ford who said, "Whether you believe you can or believe you can't, you're right." My grandmother used to repeat this phrase that will stick with me forever: "Can't never could do anything." Do you have a limiting belief around the word *try*? Is there a negative connotation getting in your way?

The results I found from this casual survey are another example of how our culture can produce limiting beliefs. These beliefs are the lies we've learned as truths, even though they are far from it. We cannot fail if we never try, and if we don't believe we'll succeed, we shouldn't bother with whatever it is we're thinking about doing. In reality, failure is a great teacher. Perhaps you harbor a different limiting belief that is inhibiting your ability to lead or succeed. Limiting beliefs keep us from moving forward. It's imperative we discover what they are.

Assumptions

Assumptions are the specific beliefs that tell us because something happened in the past, it will happen again. Assumptions are concocted stories rooted in history, and we mistakenly believe they are valid predictors of the future. We can hear the indicators of assumptions in the broad statements people make—the *everybody, always, never, nothing* statements. Assumptions often get coupled with judgments.

For example, if someone displayed passive aggressive behavior in the past, we could make the assumption that the same person will act that way all the time. In reality, that individual could show up differently with each encounter we have with him or her. Assumptions limit our ability to move forward and strengthen relationships with those around us.

INTERPRETATIONS

Interpretations are the stories we tell ourselves about someone else (or a situation) without having all the information at our disposal. These inner critics are clever. They don't stop with our brains; they enter our hearts, too. In addition to our negative thoughts, we all have negative feelings and emotional hot buttons. Our emotions are only indicators of how we are doing at any given moment of time. Unfortunately, some leaders are led by their emotions and fail to gather all the information necessary to assess a situation correctly. They make interpretations.

We expect things to be a certain way, so we don't seek out clarity or more information when we should. In many cases, particularly in the workplace where we are in relationship with a variety of people, those around us are not thinking the same way we are thinking. This can create conflict.

Brené Brown also talks about these stories in her research. The question she begs her readers and coaches to ask is, "What story are we telling ourselves?" She teaches us to recognize that these stories are based on our limiting beliefs and a lack of information. They are fairy tales that produce reactions.

There is a difference between reactions and responses. Reactions are driven by our feelings, impulses, and instincts. Responses are driven by our choices, values, and visions. We must do what we can to avoid having knee-jerk reactions. We can minimize these inner critics if we respond to others with curiosity rather than emotional reactions. We can reform our interpretations by asking questions and seeking clarity.

GREMLINS

Painful thoughts and feelings we experience in childhood, if left unchecked, prompt us to write stories deep inside ourselves. They become embedded in who we believe we are. Sometimes, these stories have been on repeat for so long we cannot seem to snag a different ending. These stories–the ones that specifically tell us we are not good enough in some way–are our biggest inner critics. They are called our gremlins.

Personal and Executive Coach, Rick Carson, first published his book, *Taming Your Gremlin*, in 1984. Ironically, that was the same year the movie *Gremlins* was released. My mentors and teachers used the phrase "taming your gremlins" throughout my pursuit in becoming a leadership coach. It was with a slightly different perspective than what Rick Carson taught in his book, but the foundational idea is that we have these inner voices–demons–that tell us these lies.

Our gremlins are born from pain or trauma from earlier in our lives, and they block forward progress because we lose confidence in our abilities. These deep voices tell us–sometimes loudly–that we are doing something that is either stretching us into arenas outside our comfort levels or that is similar to an event that caused pain in our past (embarrassment, shame, hurt, etc.). They're intrinsic warning flags. The thing is, they are no longer as valuable to us as they used to be since our past is, well...in the past. Our gremlins cannot tell the difference between what happened to us in our childhoods and the situations we experience in the present. This shaming self-talk, reinforced by the lies we learned about ourselves as children, are like broken records in our minds.

Some of my gremlins include the idea that I am not worthy of connection or love, and this idea stems from the inner voice that tells me I am not good enough to rise through the ranks of a company. I used to fear that someday, someone would realize that about me–that I wasn't good enough to be in the role I was in.

Another gremlin I used to entertain was the feeling that I was invisible or insignificant. These stories were there to protect me from past events and hurts, but as I matured and moved into new relationships and roles, I needed to understand that I was worthy (and still am!). Gremlins are the internal whispers that create self-doubt and shame, so they are the most damaging of the inner critics.

After I discovered what my gremlins, assumptions, and interpretations were, I learned how to recognize and handle them in a way that would set me up for success as a leader.

> "Winning the war of words inside your soul means learning to defy your inner critic." (Steven Furtick, Pastor and Author)

Inner critics are dangerous and limit our ability to see the options in front of us. We created most of them, but clearly our gremlins exist to protect us from future hurt. All this is to say that our inner critics can run deep. We, as leaders, need to spend some time to get to know ourselves. If we cannot quiet or negate our inner critics, they will disrupt our relationships and our ability to lead well.

We must learn how to recognize our critics, confront them, and repurpose them to help us move forward rather than hinder our progress. The more responsibility we gain in advancing leadership roles, the more important it becomes to operate from a place of positivity and truth. The further we rise through an organization, the more our behavior dictates what is acceptable for others to do. Executive and senior leaders set the culture and tone of the workplace. Leaders drive outcomes. So, how do we do this?

There is a fantastic book by Don Miguel Ruiz called *The Four Agreements*. If you have not picked it up, I encourage you to do so. I enjoyed it tremendously, and it's a quick read. The author outlines four simple ways to live life to the fullest. They are:

- Be impeccable with your words.
- Don't take anything personally.
- Don't make assumptions.
- Always do your best.

I would take these commandments a bit further than our own personal and private arenas and aim to lead by these four agreements in every arena in which we find ourselves. If we do, we will be leading with our strengths and passions and minimizing the inner critics (especially the gremlins) that distract us from our goals.

Founders, senior leaders, and presidents are only granted a handful of times to leave an impression on the people who work with them. These are the high-risk and high-reward leadership positions. We are what we do, not what we want to do, so it's imperative to conquer self-mastery to set the stage for personal, professional, team, and organizational success.

Once a leader has battled with the weapon of self-mastery and harnessed the inner critics, the next tool of the trade is waiting. Are you ready? If so, let's look at forging the second weapon for successful leadership–communication mastery.

~ 8 ~
FORGING WEAPON #2:
COMMUNICATION MASTERY

IN ANY GROUP or organization, if leaders who have failed to reach self-mastery try to move information through a group of people or an organization, the message will fall apart. If messages fall apart, no leader is successful. Simon Sinek, visionary and entrepreneur, said, "Great leaders don't blame the tools they are given, they work to sharpen them." In the previous chapters, we took a dive into the mastery of *self*. Now, we will take a look at one of two weapons related to the mastery of *we*, and the first one we will sharpen is communication mastery.

In this next story, self-mastery was the first weapon I drew to effect change in one of my working relationships. Communication mastery was the second, and it was the weapon that made all the difference. It shows if we don't sharpen each weapon in order, we will struggle to become great leaders.

I was new to leadership when I met Cheryl. Well, as a nod toward confidentiality, we'll call her Cheryl. Cheryl was born and raised in another country. She had done her graduate work in Canada and was not only fluent in English, but she understood much of western culture–or so I assumed. Perhaps the best word to describe Cheryl's workplace mannerisms and personality would be scientific. Her work was organized, her thoughts were logical, and her plans were detailed. Cheryl was an excellent subject matter expert (SME) and a valuable employee.

After a re-organization and my choice not to backfill a role left me with no middle leader for a year, Cheryl started working directly under me. I had always made certain assumptions about Cheryl–that she understood American colloquiums, we shared a common workplace language, and she was comfortable enough around me to communicate openly, to name a few.

I was wrong.

Cheryl and I collided for several months. Frustration grew between us as I falsely believed we had achieved understanding while she continued to feel work was chaos. She never pushed back or had many questions during our conversations, so I assumed all was well when they ended. All was not well.

The issue, I soon discovered after much self-reflection, was that I was making judgments without asking for more information, and I was not listening with a critical ear. I immediately set out to remedy our working relationship. Number one on my list was to move from phone calls to video calls (or in-person meetings when able). This helped our communication tremendously. I had not realized how much our native languages and cultures were impacting our ability to understand each other. We used white boards and each other's body language to help us decipher the other's meaning.

I learned Cheryl's culture and faith taught her to hold senior leaders in high regard and treat them with such an elevated level of respect that she felt uncomfortable challenging me when she disagreed with what

I proposed. I learned to pause, or continue to ask questions if she was silent. I learned a lot of things about myself, cultural differences, and especially communication.

The bottom line is that leaders must not make any assumptions about understanding. Cheryl and I assumed we understood each other, and the truth is that rarely happens the first time something is communicated, even between those from the same culture. It's the reason face-to-face conversations are so critical. We need the back-and-forth replay and confirmation.

This story is also an example of why we should follow up with emails to confirm understanding, and even after those emails are sent, it is wise to periodically check-in with others to ensure there was, in fact, understanding. Leaders must be open and prepared to have several rounds of communication on the same topic before everyone has clarity.

The picture my mind creates when I think of communication is a bridge we use to support and transport ourselves while building relationships. Communication is the mechanism that connects people. And, we know that mechanisms can break; bridges can collapse. If we don't master communication, we will not have understanding with others, and our relationships can break down, too.

As I was learning how to lead successfully, my coaches and mentors taught me to put myself out there–speak my mind. Our voices are not typically things we give a lot of thought or credence to, yet as children, speaking is one of the earliest developmental milestones. Children become very skilled at speaking truth, don't they? Somehow, as we mature, many of us lose that ability to voice our thoughts, concerns, feelings, and opinions. If we don't give voice to these things, we will never be understood.

As I've emphasized throughout this book, voicing our opinions, suggestions, and values requires courage. The flip side of communication is the act of seeking to understand others. Listening to others as they voice their opinions, suggestions, and values requires courage *and* curiosity.

Unleashing our curious minds is a good approach to take as we strive to communicate well. Just as children learn to clearly voice their thoughts and desires, they are also extravagantly curious by nature. They ask questions. Just one word, *why,* exhausts their already weary parents when it's used 50,000 times per day as children seek to understand. In the same way, great leaders constantly ask questions as they seek to understand the people, challenges, and opportunities around them.

Curiosity helps us fend off our tendencies to judge and assume. It pushes us to learn more by forcing us to take a keen interest in someone else. Curiosity provides that connection–or bridge–that helps us move from "self" to "we."

With this foundational knowledge about communication, courage, and curiosity in mind, I have compiled my top four recommendations for improving communication through courage and curiosity. I call them the ABCD's for mastering communication (for us to remember it should parallel the childlike pursuit to find meaning around us):

A. Ask the Audience.

Who is on the other side of that bridge we're traversing? With whom do we want to connect? If we want to get to know our audience (team members, peers, family, friends), we must do some detective work. Discovery always starts with questions. *What is this person or group's preferred style of communication? How do they want information from me? How can they communicate with me in a way that will facilitate my understanding of their positions?*

As a leader in the business world, I intentionally discussed communication with each of my staff members. *If you have an important or time-sensitive request or question for me, text and IM (instant messaging) are best. Next up would be a phone call. If you want my attention for an urgent matter, do not use email. Oh, and about emails—if it doesn't fit in the preview screen, call me.*

My opinion is that email is not communication; it's documentation. Everyone I worked with knew that I preferred face-to-face or voice-to-voice communication with a follow up email to summarize and validate our discussion. They also understood my habit of checking in (or inspecting) was to ensure understanding and not as a means of over-managing. I was able to build trust when I was open and collaborative.

I also gave my team members a general framework for the "what" of communication. *What works best for me as I seek to understand your need or suggestion is to tell me what I need to know (relevant background), tell me what the issue or challenge is, and then tell me what you need from me to handle the situation.* This provided them with a clear outline of the information I needed to support them. Then, as leaders, we must validate what we've heard from others. We must ask more questions. Courage is called forth when we open ourselves up by saying, "I don't understand. Please clarify."

B. Ban all Judgment.

This is likely the most challenging part of communication. It requires the foundation of self-mastery, and I do mean "mastery." Each of us places a value on the things around us—words, behaviors, beliefs, personality traits, appearance...the list goes on. It doesn't matter whether we are categorizing something as good, bad, or neutral; we are rendering judgment.

In fact, most neuroscientists would agree that over ninety percent of our behaviors are generated without our conscious effort. They are a matter of habit. If this is the case, we may want to hit the pause button on those first-impression judgments before we act upon them. So, what do we do during this "pause?"

I have learned a critical skill in leadership that has helped me ban *most* of my judgments. I've learned about perspective. Hitting pause and gaining perspective can change everything. We're often conditioned in this society, particularly in the workplace, to make decisions quickly. Many times, we do so without exploring more information or a new perspective to gain a fuller understanding of what we're seeing, hearing, or experiencing. Worse, as we just learned from science, we quickly act upon those snap judgments.

When someone disagrees with us or somehow makes our lives more difficult, it's not usually about us. Sometimes it is, but it's sometimes about his or her challenges or struggles. Taking the time to realize this is called depersonalizing or detaching. It's continuing to ask for more information in order to give ourselves more time to uncover underlying issues.

This is called reframing. When we reframe, we try on a different perspective and understand the other person is simply solving a problem in a different way than we might choose to solve it. Often, we forget that those in the arenas with us are our team members, family members, and friends. We're all on the same side. We're fighting for a common goal. Leaders must remember others may simply be using different weapons to get the job done. It is imperative we put down our own weapons long enough to determine if others' weapons are just as valuable and effective. This takes courage.

When we master the ability to pause, we can forever affect the health of the relationship we are pursuing or maintaining. When we can detach ourselves from our seemingly innate predisposition to judge, we can choose to be observant and curious instead. We may only have milliseconds to make this choice–the choice to pause–but it's critical for clear and efficient communication and for avoiding premature judgments.

C. CRITICAL AND ACTIVE LISTENING.

This may seem like a 180-degree turn from "ban all judgment" to now "listen with a critical ear." Making judgments during listening is often considered a barrier to understanding, and there is truth in that as we've seen above in part "B" of the ABCD's of Communication.

Active listening is an act of validation. You're telling the other person that you think you have understanding. Often, active listening involves a short back-and-forth conversation, repeating or summarizing what the other person has told us. A good way to ensure this has happened is by saying, "Let me play that back to you to make sure I understand."

Critical listening is moving past the sense of hearing to engage with our ears and our brains. It's hearing what is not actually said. Critical listening involves thinking, but it's also intuitive. It results in making connections between what we know from our own experiences and perspective with what the other person is telling us from his or her own unique vantage point. It's rendering judgment *after* the pause for understanding and digging deeper for clarity.

Critical and active listening both seek out the good aspects of every idea and opinion.

> "Courage is what it takes to stand up; courage is also what
> it takes to sit down and listen." (Winston Churchill)

Finally, listening is a rational process. If we are caught up in our emotions, we are limiting our ability to successfully listen for understanding. The way you engage with others and how you manage your inner critics creates your attitude. If you let your critics take over, you will limit your ability to see options and close down the ability to reframe. Look at that: Self-mastery is at play in this "C" of the ABCD's of communication as well.

★   ★   ★

A day came in my leadership career when I needed to fill a temporary position on my team, and my leader asked me to consider one of my long-time mentees for the role. Let's call her Angela.

Angela ended up as one of three finalist candidates after the first couple rounds of interviews. She was an experienced executive level director with a marketing background. Angela was proud, extroverted, and relational. I knew her well through our mentoring relationship.

As part of our typical hiring process, I asked a few of my team members to interview the finalists for "fit" on our team while I interviewed for skill set and expertise. Angela interviewed well with me, and I realized I wanted her for the role. Her skills were impeccable, and she had some experience that the other candidates did not possess.

Unfortunately, my team members were not as impressed with her outgoing personality. Under concerns she might not be vulnerable or cooperative, they preferred one of the other two finalists. I took all the information I had acquired, and I made the decision, much to my team's displeasure, to hire Angela.

I met with my team to discuss my choice and allow them to give voice to their disappointment and apprehension. And, were they ever upset! I listened to their concerns. Some were quite honest with their hesitation. Their attitudes said, "Why the hell did we even interview if you knew who you wanted to hire?" Obviously, I had modeled direct and clear communication with my team, and I appreciated it in return.

I explained I did take into account their feedback; I had just made the decision to go a different direction. It was one of those leadership battles we all must engage in during our tenures as leaders–to go against popular opinion for the good of the team or business. I did ask them to support my decision and Angela. I continued our conversation until they gained some clarity. They didn't have to agree with it, but I wanted to ensure they understood it.

The short of it is that Angela was hired and she prospered. In fact, our team prospered. She created a fun environment and drew creativity and innovative solutions out of her team members. Several of them even came to my office in the months that followed and affirmed my choice to hire her.

*   *   *

This is an example of courageous leadership. This is what it looks like to communicate well and listen with a critical ear, to gather all the information you can as a leader, and be transparent and honest with those around you. It's also a story that shows how kindness trumps niceness and leads us into the final step of forging weapon number two, the "D" of my Communication ABCD's.

D. DON'T BE NICE. BE KIND.

Sometimes, leaders are tempted to be nice, rather than kind. Kindness is based in appreciation and respect. It's caring for others in an authentic way, honoring both their values and yours. Being nice is based in accommodation and people pleasing. It's cordial and complimentary, but it's not always truthful. If leaders are nice, they could be compromising self to avoid disagreements with others. This is bad. Successful leaders are not nice; they are kind.

To be successful leaders, we must make every effort to avoid creating or perpetuating the two types of environments in our arenas that disrupt communication most. The first environment we want to avoid is the one where we are nice and agree with others in order to preserve peace or make friends with those around us. We do no one any favors by agreeing in the room and then disagreeing later at the water cooler. The nicer we are, the more unlikely we are to reach that deeper core of understanding with the people around us.

This type of behavior will only build distrust among those around us. On some level, we are surrendering what we really want or need in order to accommodate someone else. This takes us back to authenticity and sacrificing our true selves in order to preserve relationships. It doesn't work. Over time, those relationships that are not built on the foundation of authenticity will crumble. If our words and actions are not aligned, we cannot align with others on any level. No one will know what to expect from us, and our words will hold no value. For this reason, being nice also inhibits our ability to move up the leadership ladder since our words and actions do not match. People notice those kinds of discrepancies.

The second environment successful leaders want to avoid generating or supporting is the hostile environment where judgments are rendered immediately and even publicly. It's the environment that allows no room for the pause–no digging for understanding but supports flippant reactions and dissention. This type of environment causes those around us to fear disagreeing with us at all. Intimidating behavior tears down the bridge to healthy and productive relationships faster than any other. People cannot communicate well when they are fearful of our reactions to their opinions, mistakes, and feedback. One of our basic needs is to feel safe. If we don't create a safe environment, we can't expect people to thrive. Maslow's Hierarchy of Needs puts safety just after physiological needs, such as food, water, and air to breathe. Safety includes security of environment and workplace.

We now know what we want to avoid, so what type of environment do we want to *create*? Great leaders foster environments that are open, professional, and respectful. We want people to feel safe when communicating not only their ideas, but also their errors and needs. We want environments where people feel secure and will tell us what we need to know, whether we will like it or not. Kindness goes a long way in helping to build an arena where respectful communication flows effectively and efficiently.

In my opinion, our society expects "nice," particularly from female leaders. I have found that I am the most challenged as a leader with being kind versus being nice when I am engaged in performance management. In these situations, I am striving to provide honest feedback to a staff member about the need to raise his or her game.

Sometimes performance management is about stretching staff members to grow, and other times, it is about advising staff members on the areas where they are not meeting expectations. Giving this second category of feedback is always a challenge. It is important that we are heard and understood. It can be hard to validate understanding in these situations.

Think about a time when you received bad news. It is not unlike having a cupful of cold water thrown in your face, and we tend not to hear much for a while afterwards. For some people, this can be a few seconds. For others, it can be a few days. I find this varies based on how self-aware people are. The nicer we are in these situations, the less likely someone is to understand our feedback–to "get it."

*   *   *

I remember a time when I needed to have this type of conversation with a staff member of mine. Keep in mind, these should not be off-the-cuff conversations. We can't just wing them. We need to prepare, but we also need to make sure we are giving feedback as close as we can to any event that may have transpired. In this instance, I was faced with a staff member who was not meeting expectations. This individual was someone who joined my team as the result of an acquisition, and I was thrilled to have her. Based on her file, she was a top performer and someone who knew how to get sustainable results. She came to the team to fill a role that required a great deal of attention to detail, the ability to navigate horizontally in the business, and the insight to reduce the amount of cost in our process (drive efficiency).

Within the first few months, I knew something was wrong. My peers were frequently surprising me (and we know how well that goes) with feedback that my team was disruptive, and they weren't getting the results the businesses needed. As I began to dig down and ask questions, I discovered this new staff member didn't know what she was doing. She flat-out did not know how to do the job. My challenge was two-fold. She was new, and she had always received great performance feedback. Now, she was failing. I had been managing people long enough to know that if this was not resolved quickly, she would have to leave this job.

I had a conversation with her in our next weekly call. It went something like this:

"Deb (name changed), we've been working together now for a few months, and I would like to check in with you. I want to share my observations and give some feedback. During our conversation, I would also like you to let me know what I can do to help you. Okay?"

"Yeah, sure. What do you want to know?"

"I would like to know how you are settling in and get a sense of what challenges you might be experiencing."

"I'm good. Everything is going well. I feel like I am doing a really good job."

"I'm curious–how did you come to that conclusion?"

With this "how" question, I was attempting to understand if this was a skill problem (which is what I had hypothesized) or a motivation issue.

In the interest of being concise, I chose to be frank with Deb and provided her with the feedback I had received from others and my own observations. I was direct, but kind.

"Deb, you and I are not on the same page about your performance thus far. Here are my observations: [I gave specific examples, alternative actions, and the alternative result.] In addition, the feedback from the teams you support is troubling. Their perception is that we are not supporting them, and our approach is being perceived as disruptive."

I then stopped and listened.

★   ★   ★

At this point, our staff members will either respond or shut down. If she has something to say, listen and thank her for her perspective. Acknowledge her point of view. There may not be any new information that will change the situation, but we still need to allow our staff to feel heard.

Next, we need to let our staff member know we believe this is a set back and something that we are willing to help them turn around. My approach in these situations is to always partner with the person with the full expectation that they can and will improve. I work with my staff, even within that first meeting, to outline and schedule the next conversation. We agree to put the plan on paper and begin immediately. Following the conversation, as the leader, we must send a follow up email. In that email, we summarize the conversation and close with a statement of confidence that says we will support his or her improvement.

The plan is our staff member's responsibility. As leaders, we are there to support them and mentor (coach) them where we can. It is not our job to do the work for them.

The kindest thing we can do for those who work for us is to let them know where they stand in regards to their performance, whether it's good or bad. We need to excel at giving honest, kind feedback in the moment. Kindness is speaking respectful truth.

We all survive or fail as a team. It's the same way with families, small groups, or community teams. Sometimes it's not easy to say the kind (honest) thing. If we choose nice over kind, the reality is: We are being unkind. As leaders, we must use kindness to deliver the tough messages. People will respect that. They will respect us.

What do these ABCD's do for us as we strive to become great leaders? When our communication is clear, courageous, and based in curiosity, we build trust with others. In an arena built upon trust, people will begin to understand each other's language. We will share common stories. We have experienced successes and battled through failures together. We form memories and rely on these growing relationships. All of a sudden, we realize we have established a sort of shorthand to use with each other. Once we get to this point, business moves forward quickly.

Admittedly, this takes time. It won't happen overnight. Famed author, Leo Tolstoy, once claimed, "The two most powerful warriors are patience and time." There will be mistakes. The bridge may need to be repaired from time to time, but ongoing maintenance is the key.

By the way, as leaders, it is our responsibility to communicate well; it's not the other way around. We are the ones creating the environment. We must establish a culture that is safe. This creates the positive workplace we all want, and it starts with self-mastery followed by communication mastery.

Communication is that bridge that takes us from knowing ourselves to building relationships and teams. Once we've crossed the bridge and we're on the other side, it's time to sharpen another weapon. It's the second skill we need to hone for the story of "we." It's the weapon of relationship mastery.

~ *9* ~
FORGING WEAPON #3:
RELATIONSHIP MASTERY

THE SECOND TOOL we're required to sharpen in the mastery of *we* is learning how to master relationships. Excellence in communication paves the way for building trusting and lasting relationships in every arena we face. This weapon, called Relationship Mastery, is the one leadership mentors and researchers point to as one of the most difficult for *transitioning* leaders to hone. This could be because they have not forged the weapon of self-mastery, and their inner critics still rule their choices.

Leaders will be required to conquer specific relationship hurdles when moving from individual contributor roles (where we lead ourselves) to leading others. There are equally challenging skills to master when moving from one level of leadership to the next, since the expectations and accepted behaviors will be different at each milestone. Even seasoned leaders will have to make adjustments in the area of relationship building as they move throughout their careers.

Before we get further into sharpening this weapon, it's important to define relationships for the purpose of this chapter. I will be referring to the relationships we have in the workplace with those other than the individuals who report to us. Relationship mastery involves building relationships first with our peers, leaders, and colleagues.

Building these relationships is a big picture skill for any leader. It's the ability to work across the organization–both horizontally and vertically–to learn about the interconnectedness of everyone involved in the business. There is no one team that can be successful without the work of the other teams. It's a leader's job to understand and communicate that interconnectedness.

There are three internal "thought" opponents leaders must battle when it comes to relationship mastery. They are the adversaries of distance, dislike, and competition. Let's dig deeper.

I DON'T KNOW YOU

We live in the digital age–a time when many of us work from a remote location and use technology to stay connected with our teams and share our work. In fact, 50% of workers hold a job that is compatible with at least partial telework and approximately 20-25% of the workforce teleworks with some regularity. In order to be a successful leader in this culture, there are some specific battles we must win. The key battle is to build rapport and to be interested in not only the work, but also in the people doing the work–learning who they are, what is going on in their lives, and what they are passionate about.

I worked from home for decades. There's nothing like getting out of bed, getting your coffee, forgoing the makeup routine, and starting your job with your hair in a ponytail or pressed down under a hat. (Men, I'm sure there are benefits for you as well!) I earned the right to do this over many years of building relationships face-to-face. Leaders and employees alike have to earn the right to work remotely.

Distance is a formidable opponent of strong relationships. Proximity is crucial to understanding for any relationship, particularly work relationships. Some big reasons for this are our ability to use body language to find meaning, reading facial expressions to validate spoken words, being considerate to those in front of us, and our use of pleasantries and small talk to acknowledge our humanness.

Truth be told, we interpret emotions in people we know much differently than in people we don't know. For example, I know that my friend's scowl is not indicative of anger but rather of deep thought. When we get to know our peers, we're better able to discern their thoughts, feelings, and intentions and avoid incorrect assumptions that can inflame a difficult situation.

If we don't get to know our colleagues–the other leaders in the organization–and understand how our team goals align with their teams' goals, we all fail. We are all interdependent, and our success relies on the success of the whole. It may be a slow death, but make no mistake, the business will not survive with fragmented functional units operating in vacuums. In a keynote speech at The Drucker Institute, *Good to Great* author and management guru, Jim Collins, shared about the "Golden Rule" lesson he learned from his mentor, Dale Carnegie: *Don't be interesting; be interested.* It's his best advice for building relationships in leadership. Rather than trying to win over everyone, get to know everyone else first. Everyone has a story. Find out what it is, and you'll be well on your way to solving the "I don't know you" enemy of relationships.

When I worked in corporate America, one of most productive practices I used (and still get great feedback about to this day) was an icebreaker activity I called, "Who's Who in the Zoo and What Do

They Do?" Here was the gist of it: I had a standard set of slides, and the first one read, "Who am I?" The next one read, "Who's my team?" and the last one said, "What do we do?" The key was with the first slide because people could not use words, only pictures. It was similar to the collages we created in grade school. This forced the presenter to tell a story. It helped the team members understand each other in a completely different way. It was an easy exercise to implement and was also effective when I asked members of other teams to do this when they came to talk to my staff. I suggest as a leader, you consider implementing something similar.

As I've said, this is the digital age. So, it's quite simple to bridge distance gaps with video conferencing tools like WebEx, Skype, Zoom, and other platforms. We must be willing to get on camera. I know–it's unfortunate. However, being able to see and interact with our peers and the leadership circles above us is critically important to gaining trust and building rapport. Video calls and the occasional trip to the other city, state, or country allow us to convey authenticity in ways we can't over the phone. There is a term used in politics that speaks to the importance of this. It's called pressing the flesh, and politicians do it for a reason. It works. When we can see, feel, and speak with people face-to-face, they feel heard, respected, and understood.

I DON'T LIKE YOU

Meaningful and close relationships are the key to happiness. This is not new information; however, we often forget it applies in the workplace, too. Happiness and loyalty go hand-in-hand. We spend such a large portion of our time at work. It takes up the majority of our waking time, so it's important we find happiness at work. I believe we all need a close friend at work, someone in the cheering section during our battles. We all need a friend to celebrate successes with and lean on during times of defeat. In fact, Gallup completed a recent study that showed "...for women and men having a best friend at work leads to better performance. For example, our employee engagement database shows that a mere two of out 10 U.S. employees strongly agree they have a best friend at work. Yet, by moving that ratio to six in 10, organizations could realize: 36% fewer safety incidents, 7% more engaged customers, [and] 12% higher profit."

If you don't have a best friend at work, find one. As a leader, encourage those around you to connect with others in the workplace. It matters.

On the other side of the arena will always be an individual we just don't like, an enemy if you will. Whether our personalities clash, the lenses through which we see and work are vastly different, or our personal and departmental goals conflict, we will run into others who rub us the wrong way. Yes, it happens. We cannot like everyone, and everyone won't like us. This fact doesn't devalue this individual (or you).

How do we work alongside these peers whom we dislike? How do we build these difficult relationships? There is a solid truth to stand on–people respond well to those they know *and* those who treat them right. We don't have to like people to treat them well. Everyone has an intrinsic value we can acknowledge and respect. It's imperative we find it in those with whom we dislike and verbalize it.

I'm not suggesting we go have a beer or cup of coffee with them. We're not in preschool anymore–the place where everybody is our friend. The objective is to build a relationship that will get the work of the business done. Just because we don't like someone does not mean her or she is not performing the job. It's tough, but we must refrain from confusing incompetence with dislike. Find that common goal and hang on to it. We can establish what's in it for them and what's in it for us. If we're working for the same company, we have at least one common goal–the mission of the business.

There may be other, indirect commonalities. One of the most successful ways to build a relationship with someone we don't like is to find a shared goal. It may be bottom-line based, such as layoffs or any number of other business shortcomings that we're both trying to avoid.

Admittedly, some of our peers (or even leaders) may be those who simply show up for the paycheck or the prestige. Their heads and hearts are not aligned with the mission or strategic goals. They've quit inside, and it shows. It is difficult to find common ground with them. Not everyone is going to live up to our expectations, and that can get us emotionally charged. We can't force people to be engaged, and while we need to make the effort, at some point we need to know a lost cause when we see it. These individuals cannot hinder our own growth and success.

It gets messy when our emotions get tangled up in our relationships with those we don't like. Conflict almost always stems from judgment. Remember, pausing and banning judgment is critical to communication with these individuals. Likewise, communication is key to building rapport and respect. We can be successful leaders, building relationships at all levels and with all types of people with detached curiosity and respect.

I DON'T WANT TO HELP YOU

When we fail to value lateral and vertical relationships outside our own department or team, we end up working in silos, and our teams don't appreciate the bigger purpose for which they work so hard. One of the top reasons leaders ignore relationships with peers, colleagues, and other higher-level leaders within the organization is competition. We all sense the importance of competition in order to rise through the journey of leadership. However, competitive spirits can inhibit leaders from building and maintaining successful relationships. In fact, I firmly believe competition within the workplace is lethal to relationships.

At a certain level, everyone is looking to take the next step up, so people don't want to admit failure or a lack of understanding because they want the next rung on the ladder. This truth is ten-fold for peers at the leadership level. Higher management positions are more difficult to attain since there are typically fewer available. Mistakes are more visible, and depending on the environment, perhaps less tolerable.

So, what can we do? We can show up and provide our peers with a service. When we come to a place in relationships where we're feeling competitive with peers, we can choose to think differently. It's always a choice. It's that perspective word again. We can choose to think less about scarcity and more about abundance. Fundamentally, I believe this is the right approach to use to overcome negative thinking and competitive energy. In fact, any other approach (sarcasm, manipulation, ignoring other teams, selfishness, pride, fear-based tactics) takes more energy. We end up withholding critical information, working in silos, tearing down bridges of communication, and all that secrecy propels the competitive spirit forward. We end up doing harm to the business in very subtle ways that chip away at the foundation of success. If we chip long enough, the business will fail.

The truth is, we're all on the same team. Competitive edge within a company is not what's important; it's what's outside the organization that counts. If competition festers on the inside, we're not focused on the same goals–team and business success. Our role as leaders is to drive the organization forward. We can't do that when we're competing with our peers. In fact, we end up dividing the company.

Patrick Lencioni is a team management expert, business leader, and author whom I follow and respect. His book, *The Five Dysfunctions of a Team,* is a great resource and one I recommend for all leaders. He describes a reality I have found to be both fascinating and accurate. Every leader has two teams: We have a primary team and a secondary team. Here's the interesting part: Our primary team is our peer group. This may come as a surprise to some. It did for me. We are conditioned to think and act as if the group of direct reports within our functional unit is our primary team. It's where all the emphasis is placed. We must start to reframe our thinking about who is really on our teams.

If we go back to the mission of the organization, every leader's job is to drive the organization forward. This is what we've all agreed to accomplish. It's what we get paid to do! To do that, we have to partner with every business unit–all the other leaders–in order to make that happen. The sales department isn't going to be successful if they aren't working in tandem with the marketing or finance departments, even if it has the top salesperson in the country. Our secondary team is the group of people who report to us, and they know when we are not unified with our peers. There is a trickle-down effect, and productivity and morale are grossly affected.

So, what does all this mean for us? It means we need to answer for our misdirected competitive natures. We need to think and act differently toward our colleagues in leadership roles throughout the organization.

Thankfully, there is a great solution, and it was summed up by one of the greatest salesmen in business:

> "You will get all you want in life if you help enough other people get what they want." (Zig Ziglar, Author, Salesman, and Motivational Speaker)

People do things for people they like, and they don't do things for people they don't like. Zig Ziglar was correct. If you want to be successful, help others be successful first. We all want colleagues who will rally around us when we fail. We want comrades who will encourage us rather than insult us. Not surprisingly, everyone else around us wants the same thing. If we can have a win-win philosophy rather than a win-lose mentality, there is enough success around for everyone to enjoy.

I once had a uniquely brilliant leader. Every year, he forced all the leaders reporting to him to sit down with each other and build inter-departmental goals. We had to agree on these shared goals and present them to the organization. For example, what did sales need from operations to deliver on their objectives and vice versa? He understood (and taught to all of us) that we're inter-dependent. We can all make a difference, succeed, and best of all, do it together.

With all this information about relationships in mind, it's now time to uncover another naysayer in the stands. These individuals seem to want no part of you or your team's success. It's time to pick up this newly forged weapon and battle our outer critics.

~ 10 ~
FIGHTING THE OUTER CRITIC

THERE ARE THREE types of critics, and we've already tackled the management of our inner critics in Chapter Seven. As a review, inner critics are our own limiting beliefs, perceptions, assumptions, and gremlins that are hurdles or barriers to our success. The next type of critic we will fight is the outer critic. Outer critics express unfavorable opinions about something we have done or said, or they judge our work or ideas. There are three subcategories of outer critics.

THOSE WHO DISAGREE

When our peers disagree with us, our perception can sometimes be they are in some type of conflict with us. We may start to tell ourselves a story about what is happening during the disagreement. Rather than take it at face value or seek out clarity, we might make assumptions about the motivation or reason for the disagreement.

An example of this might be if we are giving a presentation in front of our leader and peers, and someone raises a concern or disagrees with our data or idea. Perhaps a couple of peers believe what we have recommended cannot work. We start to feel unsupported and our thoughts can range from "they aren't helping me" to "they are trying to make me look incompetent." It's important to understand we are telling ourselves these stories. We should pause and ask more questions to understand the disagreement or resistance further.

In the majority of cases, those who are in disagreement with us are coming from a place of "I don't understand." In order to support our idea or recommendation, they must learn everything about it first. They want all their questions answered before they can agree it's a viable recommendation. Through various studies in human sociology and psychology, it has been determined that some people start from a more cynical worldview. This means until they are able to question the idea, test our recommendation, or take ownership of a solution for themselves, they will seemingly disagree with it, no matter its merits. It does not necessarily mean they won't agree later; it simply means they can't see the value or meaning in that moment. Less mature leaders will not support an idea–and even discount it–until it's been proven worthy. Or, they may want to participate in some way to mark it as their own. Mature leaders who have the opposite perspective, an exploratory worldview, will discuss ideas to gain clarity and understanding before judging it.

In either case, be curious. Outer critics' feedback is a warning signal that perhaps we are missing something or need to communicate differently. If we navigate that obstacle they are expressing, we might find a better solution or idea. In some cases, an outer critic is a leader or someone who is a level or two above us–a bigger power at work– who is asking us to slow down to consider all points of view. The outer critics who can ask questions in respectful ways will help us clarify our messages and be better leaders. The more people involved in an idea or decision, the more well-rounded the solution will be.

Our interpretations of these outer critics and the lack of ability to manage them are the cruxes of their impact on us. Some of our problems begin when we take all the negative feedback, criticism, or adverse behaviors from outer critics and personalize them. We internalize the junk and accept it as truth, and that is precisely when they become too much a part of our battle in the arena. Why? They've turned into our inner critics. It's important we prevent this from happening.

Here is some advice I give to my clients: Circulate your ideas and gather input from various people. If you believe someone is going to be a challenge to either the team or business's unity, invite him or her to a meeting with people who have a more supportive approach to providing input. Garner the power of the group to promote change.

THOSE WHO DEBATE AND ARGUE

This next type of outer critic is the one who disagrees with a slightly more malicious purpose. These individuals want to debate. They like it. These outer critics take a different point of view for the sake of taking a different point of view. This category of outer critics can be a hindrance to the mission of the business, because they want to engage in a constant back and forth. *The sky is blue. No, it's baby blue.* The debate is not initiated for the purpose of gaining clarity or solving problems. It's debate for debate's sake. Honestly, they think it's fun.

When we uncover this motive, we'll typically discover these individuals have a reputation for this behavior. They don't just debate with us; they go back and forth with everyone. No matter the amount of curiosity we show with these critics, we can't seem to change their minds.

For the less mature leaders, this debate can quickly escalate into an argument. We will see more arguments between peers than we will when there is a hierarchy of roles in the room. If we have a peer who is this type of outer critic, this dynamic will show up in one-on-one meetings behind closed doors, and we may not realize they are doing it right away. There are dozens of reasons for the debate. Some fear they might look incompetent or stupid. With others, this is retaliatory behavior; but, for most, it's simply who they are.

More than likely, if debaters cannot articulate why they are fundamentally concerned with an idea, change, or solution, and it turns into an emotional discussion, we've bumped up against one of their values. They feel disrespected or underappreciated in some way. These individuals may have a lower EQ and not even know what's happening inside them.

It's because of these types of outer critics that some people avoid difficult conversations or situations. Some leaders block the debater and stop communicating with them for fear it's going to turn into an argument. We must resist the impulse to brush these critics under the rug. Doing so will infect the relationship and workplace like a virus.

There are many people who believe we should avoid sharing our feelings at work. I don't agree with this. I'm not saying we should sit around a box of tissues and facilitate a support group. However, it should be more than acceptable to admit, "I'm afraid if we do that, such-and-such will happen." Or, "I really can't support that because I think our customers will be unhappy." Mature peers will be able to say these things without allowing emotion to hinder communication. Those who don't understand what they are feeling will be uncomfortable. They will get angry. Remember that anger is an unexpressed fear, and if we explore that with someone who does not wield the tool of self-mastery, it may go badly. We must tread lightly and try to get to the fundamental issue at hand (the reason for the fear). If we can't build rapport, it will be detrimental to long term relationships and the work culture.

In most cases, if someone is operating from an emotional state while we're coming from a place of logic and reason, the discussion will end up in an argument. The best thing to do to calm an argument is to acknowledge that we are in a "feelings space." The conversation is emotionally charged. To disarm someone in a heightened emotional state, we might say something to the effect of, "I think I hit a nerve. Can we talk about that?" If we show open palms and present with a calm demeanor, we may be able to make some progress and end the argument. Sometimes, if an argument gets too heated, we just have to walk away until cooler heads can prevail.

THOSE WHO BULLY

The final type of outer critic that I have identified is the bully. These individuals are master manipulators. The motivation for their negative feedback or arguments is to feel empowered or gain an advantage. It's a one-sided affair. In their efforts to further their own agendas, they collect followers (I call them minions) along the way. They believe everyone should follow them because pride and ego are usually involved.

Many times, we don't even see what is happening in our first encounters with them. They are not the kinds of bullies who push us down or throw us into the locker. It's subtle manipulation with one purpose–to get what they want for their own gain. Bullies are not trying to grow anyone or move the mission of the business forward.

A bully's rationale might say, "I'm right. You must not understand what I'm saying, because if you did, you'd know I am right." When we are engaged in this kind of conversation, we are face-to-face with a bully. The message they are communicating is *you're not smart enough to agree with me.* The reality is they might be wrong, but they won't admit it.

My suggestion (which is somewhat of a confrontational response) is to say, "Hey, I understand what you're saying. It isn't that I don't grasp your opinion or idea. It's that I disagree with it. I'd like to talk about that." It's very difficult to get bullies to appreciate a different point of view. They probably treat everyone this way. It's important to remember, it's not about us. It's about them.

Some of our bullies will come from a different area of the organization, show up in our offices, and offer us just enough information to get us to act on their behalf. They don't give us enough of the story to help us, permit us to make our own decisions, or allow us to understand the impact on the mission of the organization. Otherwise, we may not do what they want. This is the bully I refer to as the "pot-stirrer." They know they will trigger some value of ours if we have too much information, so they withhold critical details—or the whole story—so we'll agree to their plans of action. If we did know the whole story, we wouldn't be misled into doing their bidding.

With pot-stirrer bullies, it's important we ask a lot of questions. Be curious. Once we show that we aren't going to immediately act without more answers, they are forced to tell us the whole story, and they are effectively disarmed.

Then there are some bullies who show up and make the claim, "Hey, it's you and me against everyone else." Perhaps we were both hired into leadership roles around the same time. Or, we are the new leader, and they give the impression they want to help us, but in reality, they want to control us. We typically cannot negotiate with a bully. They may give us irrelevant feedback to disrupt our forward progress or get into our heads. If our peers aren't helping us but only want us to do things for them, we should carefully choose when and how to partner with them.

A bully's shield is privacy. They won't intimidate others in public. We can use this information to help us manage bullies. If we find a group or an ally to bring the idea back to the table in a meeting with three or more people, we can occasionally stop the bully's tactics. The truth is, we cannot change anyone but ourselves, and sometimes, all we can do is work around the barrier rather than try to move it.

These types of outer critics–the bullies–are rare. We won't recognize bullies until their ugly sides come out. I had a peer whom I also considered a friend, but that isn't what the relationship turned out to be. This ended up being one of those relationships that caused me to reconsider my ability to judge people.

I had worked alongside this woman for several years before the ugly crawled out. We were in the midst of a reorganization, and when the music stopped I was left without a clear position. Leadership told me I needed to apply for a new role. My friend landed a role without having to apply for it. I didn't understand it. When I inquired about it, I was told it was because there were other people qualified for the role they had pointed me toward. I had to fight for the role.

Time went by, and I was offered the new role and accepted it. While not happy with the fact it wasn't a promotion, I eventually made peace with where I landed and leaned into doing my job well. Sometimes you gotta dance to the song that's playing.

Fast-forward a year, and the president of the company retired. We get a new one in place. This time, I was asked to sit at the president's table. My friend was not, and out came the ugly, bully-like behavior.

The morning we were to move a portion of my team to her team, she said to me, "You know they are all going to be out to get you. They will work to sabotage you at every turn." I was shocked. I expected her to be happy for me. It went from shockingly bad to downright awful. She left the group shortly thereafter. You never know when a bully is going to pop up.

Bullies think they are better than us. Their goal is to shut us down. They win if it works, because they've taken a small measure of our power. When we get to certain levels in leadership, we can't complain to our leader about these individuals. Senior level executives are expected to solve problems, particularly relationship-based ones. We can't go and tattle-tell, or we will create the perception we are whining. However, we can ask our leaders for help. I've used this approach: "I'm struggling. I don't know how to work with (bully's name). I don't want you to intervene, but I would appreciate it if you coached me through this."

As leaders, we have to keep going. One mentor of mine used to say, "He's a rock in the stream. Just flow around him." I want to reiterate that bullies are rare, but they do pop up in workplaces, particularly when we are in new leadership roles. I don't share about this type of outer critic to plant fear or distrust in our relationships, but we do need to be aware they exist. The last thing we want is to be associated with a bully and be mislabeled with the phrase "not a team player" because we've been sucked into this type of relationship.

Outer critics can trip us up if we fail to change the dynamics they creat in the stadium to don't stay "above the fray", remain authentic, hold to our values, communicate, disarm, and show curiosity while seeking to understand. If we ignore the behavior or choose not to address the issues at hand, we are perpetuating an environment that will lead to our downfall. The critics will win. Yet, if we counterattack and engage in the drama, we will be fighting a different battle–the adverse reputation of being difficult to work with. If we push back too hard, our reactions give the message that we are *so right* that perhaps we're not able to collaborate or remain professional. We cannot let this happen. Our staff is watching.

We can find common ground with outer critics, but we must not stop there. No one wants to build a business on the lowest common denominator for the sake of agreement. Collaboration is critical. We shouldn't be too quick to get to an answer if we have a dissenter in the room. Sometimes, the dissenting voice is right. We shouldn't seek to quiet it or implement "the majority wins" philosophy quickly. If we do, we may be inhibiting innovation and development. Maintaining the status quo isn't the same as striving for excellence. It may provide peace, but it does nothing for growth. As leaders, we must be okay with making changes to get to the right solution.

There are specific strategies leaders can use in order to suspend any outer critic's potentially negative influence. It's important to address the behavior since outer critics who are not handled properly will ignite inner critics or become invisible critics, whom we'll learn about in a future chapter. You'll discover the strategies we discussed earlier in "Communication Mastery" go a long way in resolving behavior that stems from outer critics.

- Be kind, not nice. Don't bend so far that you break, but be respectful and flexible.
- Don't get sucked into the drama, but don't discount these individuals either.

119

- Let outer critics be heard. Listen critically.
- Acknowledge their concerns and validate their feelings.
- Get to know them. Ask questions. Be curious.
- Validate when your critic has asked a good question.
- Admit when you don't have the answers. Don't give the impression you know it all.
- Find the answers to those questions and circle back.
- Build rapport. Be interested.
- If they are bold and threatening, disarm or walk away.
- Do not engage in combative words or behaviors or give the impression there is a battle to be won (even though philosophically, there is). Embrace a healthy debate and learn something.
- Find your pause button. Take five seconds to let go of whatever inner critic is whispering in your ear.
- Realize it's your job to help outer critics understand why they are resisting and to seek understanding about their points of view as well.
- When faced with a bully, get help or seek an ally.

I have used all of these strategies–many of them in just one conversation. "You seem frustrated by something I've said or done. I'd like to understand your perspective. [Listen to their opinion.] I hear your frustration. Many people who experience [fill in the blank] are frustrated. It's understandable you're feeling this way. Is there anything else you want to share? [Offer your perspective or more information for their benefit.] What can we do to resolve this?"

In my earliest leadership years, I had the reputation of being quick to anger and difficult to work with. Obviously, I didn't like that image. (I have done a lot of inner work, and it is still an ever-present development area for me.) I worked to build rapport with the people who worked alongside me, and after time, they were able to get to know me better. They realized the negative reputation was a perception, and I was being misunderstood. We became a group of people who cared about each other, and over time, they were able to help me change the opinions of the outer critics around me.

A sure-fire way to disrupt our ability to establish a good relationship is to ask the wrong questions of our outer critics. As leaders, it's imperative we understand that what we say is important. Words hold power. While "why" questions are not inherently bad, they are not the best questions to start with when we are engaging with our peers, particularly outer critics. If we don't save the *why's* for after we have built rapport, people tend to get defensive. *Why* implies they weren't able to convey their message, and they could make the assumption that you think their ideas or solutions are wrong. We can rephrase our questions into *how*, *what*, or *where* questions, and this goes a long way in preserving trust and respect.

A great example from my past was a time when I was looking at a peer's PowerPoint presentation. It had a chart, and I wanted to know why this person decided to use that data because it wasn't exactly clear. I could have asked, "Why did you choose that data?" However based on previous experiences, I knew that question would cause this particular peer to become defensive. Instead, I asked, "What was the process you used to select this particular data set?" Another way to phrase it could have been, "What was it about this data set that you liked?" As you can imagine, my "what" question invited my coworker in for a conversation rather than forcing him to defend his work, and ultimately, we were able to build rapport with each other.

I've talked about rapport throughout the book, particularly in this chapter. It really is the key to building relationships and disarming critics. According to Daniel Goleman–whom I referenced earlier–rapport is established in three distinct ways. First, we engage someone with full and mutual attention, which is best done face-to-face. Second, we can experience body synchronicity. This is the phenomenon where we begin to unconsciously mirror each other's movements and mannerisms when we spend time together. Within the last decade, scientists and researchers discovered oscillators in our brains that affect our ability to read and respond to people. For example, when two people move toward each other for a first kiss, there are two heads coming together with no prior understanding of how they will fit together. Without these oscillators adjusting each individual's movements, the two would collide. Third, when we build rapport, we develop good feelings of mutual connection and understanding. These are not the same feelings as we find in friendships. We simply feel good. It comes from finding a harmonized way of being with one another–from being understood.

From one leader to another, if you don't have either of these books in your library (arsenal), I recommend you get them. The first is *The Collaborative Way: A Story About Engaging the Mind and Spirit of a Company* by Lloyd Fickett. It's not a story, per se, but a recipe for how to collaborate effectively and build rapport with your teams. What I like most about the book is the recommendations the authors make about communication–to develop an internal language based on these key elements: listening generously, speaking straight, being there for others, honoring commitments, and acknowledging and appreciating others.

The second book is *Silos, Politics, and Turf Wars* by Patrick Lencioni. This book is written as a fictional—but completely realistic—story about a young management consultant struggling with a common business problem. Through trial and error, he finds a simple yet innovative approach for transforming confusion and conflict into clarity and cooperation. Collaboration–not compromise–is the key. Although, there is truth to the fact we sometimes need to compromise in order to collaborate down the road. Little wins are still wins.

Finally, there are benefits to having outer critics in the workplace. I have complied a short list, but you may think of others.

Benefits of Outer Critics

- We will find better, more successful solutions.
- We may discover our blind spots and learn something about ourselves.
- We can build rapport and foster new relationships.
- We can reach an understanding we never had before.
- We can learn that we don't have to be married to certain outcomes.
- We can find new allies–build connections–to help us bring bullies to the light and manage the manipulative power of bullies.

In summary, when we allow others into our circles and share pertinent information with them, we build rapport. This is an integral part of building relationships and will help you manage outer critics whose motivations are "I don't know enough yet so I disagree" or who simply like to debate. In essence, we must handle all outer critics directly. The outer critics whose motivation is "I don't want to help you," (the bullies) will be the bolder and more threatening critics. They are engaging in scarcity thinking. With these critics, it's imperative we bring them into the light with the help of allies, or at the very least, distance ourselves so as not to be associated as one of their minions. It will take creativity and allies advocating against false reputations they might be constructing for us.

If we can effectively build relationships with our outer critics, they teach us a great deal about leadership and help us hone our communication and people skills. Think of outer critics as caution flags in our working world. If we pay attention to them, we can not only stop the criticism but also start to partner with them in the arena. In fact, outer critics can become our greatest allies as we seek to build our teams and move the business forward. As we manage our outer critics, we are not colluding with others. We are leveraging partners who will engage positively in order to fulfill the mission of the business.

Now that we've discussed relationship mastery and dealt with some of the outer critics we will face, we're ready to sharpen the final weapon for the leadership arena. It's the one most of us think about when we consider what it means to be a leader in the workplace–team mastery.

~ 11 ~
FORGING WEAPON #4: TEAM MASTERY

WE'VE LEARNED WHAT it takes to master ourselves. We stepped into the first half of the story of *we* as we reviewed communication strategies and honed the weapon of relationship mastery. It's time for forging the final weapon at our disposal, mastering the teams we lead. It's the second half of the story of *we*.

Every leader must learn to lead those under his or her direction well. There are several aspects leaders must appreciate to acquire team mastery. We will specifically discuss these three components: people management, conflict management, and managing differences.

PEOPLE MANAGEMENT

The Center for Creative Leadership published a white paper regarding major leadership challenges for FTMs (First-Time Managers). The research determined, "The challenge that was most often cited by FTMs involved the difficulties associated with moving from a coworker to a superior role and establishing one's authority in the new leadership role. More than half of FTMs (59.3%) said this is one of their biggest challenges." The authors of the white paper labeled this skill "Adjustment to People Management/Displaying Authority." I contend this is one aspect of the full weapon of team mastery.

Employee engagement is a key focus area for any business. This does not only refer to the alignment of an employee's specific skills and talents in a role, but also his or her feelings and emotional attachment to the company, the job, the culture, and the other employees within the company. Loyalty toward a workplace is not common anymore. Gone are the days where individuals retire after thirty-five or forty years of service at one company simply because it's expected. Therefore, how we manage people is critically important for positively impacting employee loyalty.

As leaders, we need to create the environment where the whole of a person is valued and respected, ensuring our teams become engaged through not only their skills, but also through their goals, visions, ideas, outputs, and relationships. Employees are not tools, but assets. They are the keys to the success of the mission of the business. When we approach people management through this lens, the byproduct is success. We experience performance at its highest level.

These days, it's important to attract the right "talent;" it's just as important to manage people effectively. While this chapter is dedicated to day-to-day leadership of teams, performance management of individuals on teams is equally as important. Our role as a leader is to choose the right members for our teams and let go of the wrong ones. Every company approaches performance management differently, and each state and industry has specific legalities to consider. For this reason, I will not get into any details here about performance management. Suffice to say, respect, feedback, openness, and accountability will go a long way in helping you be successful when managing performance. Here are my main recommendations:

- Engage your HR professionals early and often.
- Be open to how you may need to change, and what role you play.
- Be sure to recognize accomplishments more than you provide feedback or address the need for improvement.
- Never provide feedback when you're angry.

Now, let's return to the mastery of people management. What does it mean for us as leaders today to build high performing teams, particularly as new leaders moving into the role of a leader from a former role as a peer or coworker? There are several practical steps emerging leaders can take:

- Provide teams with clear goals and objectives–ones aligned with the organization's mission. Help teams see how they connect to the bigger mission.
- Be clear on the "what" part of the goal, but let the team determine the "how." I'm not recommending we tell our staff what to do and walk away. I am suggesting leaders engage in building relationships with people and through empowerment, nurturing them with development opportunities. Don't let them flounder, but help them grow.
- If you find yourself leading former peers, acknowledge the awkwardness. There's no way around it. An honest conversation can go a long way to build a new type of relationship with peers who are now direct reports. Let them have their feelings about it. Open communication is everything.

- Establish what is called "engaged detachment." You are still the partner they know you as, but they learn you are also the leader. In essence, you cannot stand at the water cooler and chat with the people who were your friends or former peers, but you can engage each individual on your team with a weekly meeting or discussion over coffee to get to know them better to build and maintain connections.

- Create small wins for your team members. Help them see the milestones along the path to the goal and celebrate with them. This will build trust and greater engagement right from the start.

- Support privacy and keep confidentiality. Trust is paramount in building relationships.

- Understand that community is not something you find; it's something you build. Create easy connections for your team members with you, each other, and between other teams. Build an environment where people don't feel isolated and where favoritism (real or perceived) doesn't exist.

Let's get into some specifics. It's important to understand that the relationship with those who were your friends will be strained. It is not easy to transition to the "engaged detachment" relationship with a former coworker-turned-direct-report who is a personal friend. I've seen these relationships fail, personally experienced this type of relationship suffering, and watched people successfully navigate it as well. It takes two exceptionally mature people to maintain this kind of a personal yet professional relationship. Candidly, I don't recommend it until you have mastered the arena of leadership. It is more likely to backfire than it is to work. For example, in over two decades of leadership, I have been successful only two times. Every other time I attempted to balance personal and professional relationships with staff, it backfired.

As leaders, we have to be both equitable and visionary. Access equals privilege in this arena, and your old friends will either actively or passively (intentionally or unintentionally) use it to gain information or favor. Subsequently, others may try to leverage your friends to manage you for what they want as well. I have watched friends of new leaders alienate the rest of the team by carrying on some kind of behavior that showcased a "favorite" status, whether it was perceived or real.

Employees and leaders within an office setting are observant. Team members see a lot of what we are doing, even if we don't realize it. They watch. They witness us meeting with certain people (or not meeting with others); they keep track of the behaviors and attitudes we display with some people versus others. I actually carry a card around with me that states, "Be deliberate. They are watching and listening to everything you say and do, even if you can't see them." It's a good reminder of this reality. Make no mistake, our direct reports will engage in dialogues at the water cooler about us. That is just how it is and we need to accept that it happens. Our place is no longer at the water cooler. Leaders must have boundaries. The key for us as leaders is to distance ourselves tactfully and professionally.

If we hear our team members start calling the leadership team "management," something is broken. Work quickly to heal it. They are distancing themselves from us and they can start blaming. They will become disengaged, make choices based on their feelings of being unappreciated, or maybe even start stirring the pot. Creating an environment where speaking up and getting clarity is encouraged. It is paramount to leading our new teams. We must design a team culture that allows for people to feel safe to share their concerns and feelings. This will allow them to speak truth to power (us). If we don't, our teams will never become high performing ones, and the mission of the business will suffer. We want people to think of us as "leaders," not "managers." Our goal is respect, not popularity or even strict authority.

As discussed in "Communication Mastery," it is important to share our preferred communication styles with our teams. It's important they know what we like and don't like and perhaps even what our "red buttons" or triggers are. We should also seek similar information from individuals when we meet with them. When we share information about ourselves, it's a good idea to do it in a group setting so we can make sure everyone gets the same level of clarity. I recommend sharing the following with them and ask how you can help them be successful.

- Discuss each of your communication styles and acceptable communication venues (email, text, phone, in-person, IM, etc.)
- Discuss each other's availability and in-office hours
- Be vulnerable and disclose your individual triggers and hot buttons, and ask about theirs
- Find out what makes them feel the most valued and appreciated
- Discuss the resources they need to do their jobs well
- Offer the opportunity for them to ask questions of you

Example for one-on-one meetings:

Schedule a meeting with each of your team members (one-on-one), and say, "I'm new in this role, and I want to understand you, your talents, your communication style, and your needs and I want you to understand more about me." Create the conversation. Be sure to stop and listen. This isn't about how interesting you are. It is about how interested you are in them. Some common items to discuss are the same items you shared with the group and how you can help them be successful as individuals.

Listening is great, but to earn credibility, we must do something with the information we gain. When we are able to create an environment where people feel heard and get to know us as their leaders, the team benefits. We begin to see our staff as people rather than workers, and they begin to trust us. When our teams trust us, they will follow our lead.

CONFLICT MANAGEMENT

Most leadership books will discuss conflict management in one way or another. Successful conflict management is a critical component of effective leadership, and it is one of the most feared challenges we must tackle as a leader. Relationships are messy. But, they are also necessary.

There are two types of conflict. One is productive conflict when diverse opinions come together to produce the best solutions to problems. This type of conflict forces us to explain our positions and viewpoints in an effort to secure the most efficient or effective strategy to move the business forward. Productive conflict allows team members the ability to freely brainstorm without fear of judgment. It fosters creativity and promotes collaboration. The more perspectives a team can gather, the better the solution they will find. In fact, productive conflict–healthy discussions–produces more unified and aligned results. A result is only a result when it is realized. If you can't get alignment and unity around an action, you will not get a result.

The other type of conflict is detrimental conflict. This is conflict that pits one person against another and rather than attempting to understand each other, creates adversity, competition, or friction. Detrimental conflict becomes personal, and people get hurt. This is the conflict our minds automatically turn to when the term "conflict management" is used in leadership or human resources arenas.

This is the reason I have never liked the term conflict. It's broad and it implies a war between two people or groups–a clash. While that idea would fall neatly into our metaphor of the arena and the battles we face as leaders, it's important to understand that conflict is more than arguments, quarrels, or disagreements. Detrimental conflict occurs when someone's values bump into (okay, sometimes they "collide") with another's values. It can also manifest when certain personality characteristics trigger a coworker's emotional buttons. Finally, detrimental conflict can even be caused by a story we are telling ourselves about a situation.

The decision about whether to speak out in opposition or not is instrumental to getting to the best answer. Not all disagreements are negative or heated. This is how good decisions are made. The disagreement becomes beneficial if we ask some of these questions:

- *What is it about this interaction that is causing me to feel in conflict with this person rather than as a partner?*
- *Am I brainstorming, sparking curiosity, or seeking to better understand this new perspective?*
- *How is holding back my comments going help or hurt the situation?*

I once heard a comedian say there were three questions he asked himself that helped to save his relationship with his girlfriend:

- Does this need to be said?
- Does this need to be said by me?
- Does this need to be said by me right now?
- If all answers are yes–speak up.

The consequences of conflict are variable. Some staff members who disagree with a position or don't accept a decision will shut down and become disengaged. Others react poorly through their choices, words, or behaviors. Still others will simply ignore the team's direction–and our directives–as they continue to do their own thing. We may even encounter people who seem to comply (on the outside), but on the inside, they are filled with disappointment and perhaps anger. With any of these situations, morale is affected, and the whole team suffers the repercussions.

Conflict management involves the ability to proactively prevent or reactively resolve disagreements, differences, or negative attitudes. It involves mitigating conflict before it even occurs, but it also includes identifying small issues before they grow into larger, problematic disputes. As leaders, our job is to create an environment for success. Workplace discord takes energy, time, and resources away from the mission of the business and the goals of our specific teams. The object of conflict management is to support the team–and the business– by helping everyone involved understand the strength found in our differences.

It is important to appreciate that conflict typically stems from the stories people tell themselves about a situation or someone else's actions or words. We all have a current reality, and sometimes our reality does not align with everyone else's...or even the truth. Oftentimes, people can become emotional when they perceive their values have been discredited, ignored, or threatened. You'll hear people say things like, "I don't feel like he respects me," "She keeps talking down to me," or "I think she's rude/he's arrogant." These descriptors are based on the story this team member has been telling himself or herself over time and they define the relationship.

There are countless strategies for managing conflict and recognizing the strengths of our differences. I believe it's imperative to lead through conflict management with the foundation of authenticity. Authentic leadership styles can derail most negative reactions, disagreements, differences of opinion, personalities, or attitudes. Authentic leadership is the practice of adaptively managing people and relationships from our core, choosing to allow our true selves to show up and serve the greatest good in any given moment. Sometimes, serving the greatest good means managing messy or complicated relationships. As we do, we overcome those unproductive consequences mentioned earlier and our teams thrive.

These are some of the practical ways we can master conflict management through authentic leadership:

- Know yourself–your values, passion, and purpose–and lead consistently through them.
- This may seem counter-intuitive, but create an atmosphere that allows for discord to take place (in a healthy way). Everyone wants to be heard. Provide a safe space for productive

communication to take place by initiating honest and authentic conversations.

- Create a common language among team members. Brené Brown, in *Rising Strong*, writes about this strategy. For example, "I will need to circle back," means, "I am not comfortable with a decision that has been made, and I need to talk about it." Ensure every team member knows the language.

- Recognize emotional outbursts as hot buttons or triggers that have been pushed, and allow time for team members to cool off. Encourage team members to avoid reacting to behaviors and instead seek to understand and address the individual's needs.

- As a leader, remain calm and if needed, detach from the situation temporarily (hit your pause button) so the emotional burden does not hinder your own communication.

- Capitalize on the conflict as you're working to resolve it by creating a learning opportunity for your team. Coach your employees to contest the opposing issues, not the people on the other side of the table. Encourage your team to recognize biases, and teach them to look for win-win situations.

- Leverage painful situations to deepen relationships and create team building experiences. Relationships can grow stronger after conflict.

All conflict is not bad. If managed well by the leader, it can create powerful teams, open up honest communication, and promote vulnerability. Conflict resolution is a valuable learning tool for building trusting relationships. It exposes the fears present in others, and if handled correctly, can create the opportunity for every member to see the strengths found in our differences and build confidence for speaking up.

Managing Differences

Every group we lead, no matter the size, will have differences. Managing and working with a wide range of people takes wisdom. The key to team mastery is to not ignore, compartmentalize, or minimize the differences. In fact, we should do the exact opposite. If we are intentional about recognizing our diversity, understanding our differences, and utilizing the strength found in these differences, we will create an environment of trust, impact, and respect. So, how do we exploit our differences in an effort to build better teams?

The first step for leaders is to create the space for people to recognize our differences in a vulnerable, yet safe environment. Many leaders use team building activities, workshops, or retreats to accomplish this. However, we don't have to set aside a formal day away from the office to undertake this step. There are numerous professional assessments available. We can invite a diversity expert or coach to provide an in-service opportunity. Many leaders hold "lunch-and-learn" training experiences. What will these types of activities uncover and why is this important?

Most people think of race when they hear the term "diversity," and while recognizing racial differences is important, there is no justice in pretending skin color is of no significance in an effort to avoid racial injustices. Maintaining an ideology of color-blindness, or a refusal to recognize how race and racism impacts the lives of individuals, is a mistake many leaders make. When leaders say we don't see race, it means we don't see the importance of one's racial identity–including the gifts and insights that come with it–or the ways that racism impacts the professional and personal experiences of our team members.

Along with race, there are cultural, age, value, and gender differences leaders must assess and appreciate. In every culture, there are basic standards of thinking and acting, and these cultural standards impact and individual's workplace values and communication. Even the choice of words we use is a form of diversity.

There are words, phrases, expressions, and jargon we all need to learn to communicate with those around us. Know this–we come to the table with biases. All of us do. Acknowledging them will help us keep them from getting in the way of building our teams. There is an online assessment available that can help uncover biases. It's called Project Implicit from Harvard University. I recommend leaders use it as tool for themselves (not to share with their teams). Some knowledge is simply for us.

I can remember trying to communicate with different functional units within an IT division. The word "build" meant different things to different groups, depending on the work they did. I had to learn that difference as a leader in the IT division.

Age plays a colossal role in a team member's perspective. It's the reason there is such an emphasis on managing through generational differences in this country. Most people now recognize five generations in today's workforce.

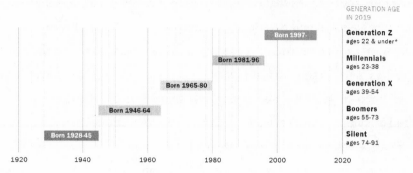

GENERATION AGE
IN 2019

Generation Z
ages 22 & under*

Millennials
ages 23-38

Generation X
ages 39-54

Boomers
ages 55-73

Silent
ages 74-91

Born 1997

Born 1981-96

Born 1965-80

Born 1946-64

Born 1928-45

1920   1940   1960   1980   2000   2020

*No chronological endpoint has been set for this group. Generation Z age ranges vary by analysis.

PEW RESEARCH CENTER

Although there are always exceptions to the norms, it is true that the generations communicate differently and have vastly different expectations and values surrounding work. There is so much information available on generational differences that I will simply say it is beneficial as leaders to continue learning more about the generations, as the workforce is constantly changing.

Value differences will certainly trigger conflict on teams. Values are deeply held beliefs that don't change easily. It's more difficult for team members to compromise a value than an opinion. These are the differences that trigger those emotional responses.

However, the leadership skill I am going to spend most of this chapter on is managing gender differences. The reason for this is that I believe it would be a disservice to write in depth about differences that I have not experienced personally. So, as a white southern female, the majority of the differences I have faced are related to being a woman in what has traditionally been a man's world. I am not emphasizing this because it is the most important or most detrimental to leadership. I am sharing because it is what I know and have experienced most often.

Gender differences are important for leaders to recognize and seek to understand. While I am a huge proponent of equality, I also recognize there are unique gifts that many female leaders possess which male leaders may not, and vice versa. Any attempt to equate gender (notice I did not use the term gender equality, for that is different) fails to recognize these powerful and differing assets. In fact, it may negate them altogether.

I'm not sure we truly understand how words can so powerfully impact someone's life. For example, look at this chart compiled after months of research on gender differences in the workplace:

Managers Use More Positive Words to Describe Men in Performance Reviews and More Negative Ones to Describe Women

Words used to describe men		Words used to describe women	
POSITIVE	NEGATIVE	POSITIVE	NEGATIVE
Analytical		Compassionate	
Competent			Inept
Athletic		Enthusiastic	Selfish
Dependable	Arrogant	Energetic	Frivolous
Confident			Passive
Versatile		Organized	Scattered
Articulate			Opportunistic
Level-headed			Gossip
	Irresponsible		Excitable
Logical			Vain
Practical			Panicky
			Temperamental
			Indecisive

IN DESCENDING ORDER OF RELATIVE FREQUENCY

SOURCE AN ANALYSIS OF 81,000 PERFORMANCE EVALUATIONS, DAVID G. SMITH ET AL., 2018   © HBR.ORG

Leadership attributes in performance evaluations are influential. They are not simply words; they can have far-reaching implications for employees and the organization itself. The language we use in performance evaluations tells us what is and is not valued in the organization. Employees learn what is respected and make choices and decisions about how they should behave in an organization based on that common language. Employees learn that opportunities to advance may be based on that common language.

> "Words are things. You must be careful, careful about calling people out of their names, using racial pejoratives and sexual pejoratives and all that ignorance. Don't do that. Some day, we'll be able to measure the power of words. I think they are things. They get on the walls. They get in your wallpaper. They get in your rugs, in your upholstery, and your clothes, and finally into you."
> (Maya Angelou)

Language isn't the only significant impact on gender in the workplace. Attitude, influenced by cultural expectations, can alter performance. "Males tend to convey more confidence than women in performance-oriented settings," writes George Washington University law professor, Charles Craver, in an essay titled, *The Impact of Gender on Bargaining Interactions*. The information was based on experiences in his classroom. "Even when minimally prepared, men believe they can 'wing it' and get through successfully. On the other hand, no matter how thoroughly prepared women are, they tend to feel unprepared." This dynamic transfers from the classroom to the workplace. As leaders, we must realize it (still) exists.

The most important step in managing differences well is to take on a posture of learning. It is important to know we all have differences. It's more important to understand what those differences mean and how they will impact our relationships–yes, even how they can improve our relationships.

Before I dive into my personal anecdotes for gender differences, you should know I was influenced by two factors. First, I grew up without a father in my life. Because of this, I never really learned how to interact with males in authoritative positions until I was knee-deep in the workplace. Second, I grew up watching and learning from a working mother. I did not realize in that era, working mothers were not the norm. I believed the bras had already been burned, so to speak. When I entered the workforce, I had no inkling there were still major hurdles to jump when it came to gender equality. My first taste of those hurdles in leadership was definitely bitter.

I already shared my experience with my conversation at the employment agency when the female interviewer told me I'd never become an accountant, let alone a leader, and advised me to learn how to type. I had chalked the whole thing up to ignorance on her part. I sort of brushed it off, never realizing that it was still, in fact, the current reality for most women in the workplace.

Later in my career, I had another profound experience. The story comes from my first leadership role, which was as the CFO at a hospital. A regional meeting of CFOs had been scheduled. I proceeded to put on my dress suit–which I didn't wear much anymore–and walked down a long hall to the conference room. I knew I looked crisp and professional. I had confidence walking in there.

The conference room itself was old and unimpressive. It smelled a bit musty, and there was the trademark hum in the background caused by the fluorescent lights overhead. There were long wooden tables, much like what you'd find at an older church, and there were no linens covering them. Mismatched chairs surrounded the tables.

Three older, white men sat around these tables. I strolled in. They immediately mistook me for somebody's secretary. Right off the bat, they asked me to serve coffee and take the minutes. My cheeks flushed. I thought, *maybe I'm not confident enough.*

In a strange turn of events, I did not fight back–unusual for me. Well, that's not completely accurate. I did respond in a passive aggressive, rebellious kind of way. I explained who I was and negotiated with them. I told them I would take minutes if one of their secretaries would type them up. They agreed. I proceeded to write with my left hand (I'm right-handed), and all the notes were ineligible. I also made really bad coffee. I chuckle now as I recall the incident.

No one ever asked me to take minutes again. No one asked me to make coffee again. Unfortunately, it was for the wrong reasons. This was my first introduction to being a female in a senior leadership role in a place and time when that was not the norm.

I don't believe the insults were intentional. The men around that table were not trying to put me in my place in any way. They fundamentally believed a secretarial job was the position I must have held, and when they learned the truth, they didn't know what to do or think. There was no malice, simply ignorance.

I became a force to be reckoned with in that CFO position and earned the respect of all three of those men in that conference room (not that it was imperative I did that). One even hired me a few years further down the road from the time this story took place. Of course, I should never have had to earn that kind of respect simply by the impression left by my heels and dress. It was the reality of that time and place, though admittedly, this kind of gender bias continues today. It may be more indirect or covert, but it's still there. The good news is that the leaders of today have the ability to change this. That's you and me.

Formality can be a hindrance. What comes to mind for me is a time when I joined a big business and was introduced to the formal dress code. At the corporate office, the dress code for women was clear. We were required to wear heels, pantyhose, a suit, and were not permitted to wear any sleeveless attire. Men were required to wear suits with ties and dress shirts. This dress code had been in place for a long time. While I watched it relax significantly over time, it was clear to me this separated more than it unified.

These formal and antiquated dress codes affect leadership and the corporate culture in ways you may not have ever realized. These dress code differences can, in fact, stimulate unconscious biases. They highlight clear gender differences within the business all the way up the ladder. Skirts and heels are somewhat limiting attire, and the choices some of my female colleagues made were more appropriate for a bar room than a boardroom. The dress code was one such "aha" moment. I am confident it was an unintended outcome of a well-intentioned policy. As leaders, we must be intentional and ensure the culture doesn't become divisive and learn that what used to be is not always what should continue to be.

Despite the turning cultural tide, men still have certain advantages in leadership. Those of you who are male may not understand or see this at first, but if you take a moment and think about what I'm sharing, you may discover it is happening today, even within your current workplaces.

Male leaders enjoy an inherent camaraderie because men continue to outnumber women in leadership roles. Females are needles in a supremely large haystack. There is no immediate camaraderie when a woman is promoted or hired into a new leadership role because there is rarely more than one of us at the table. A colleague once told me the reality for female leaders is that we need three women at any leadership table in order to be heard. I saw this play out in my journey. I've learned, if there is just one of us, we are often not heard. Two women in disagreement is perceived as a catfight. Three breaks the tie. So, for now, we still seem to need three.

In my past experience, there were dozens of instances when I voiced an opinion, recommendation, or concern and received no acknowledgment from the group. However, minutes later, when a male peer made the same recommendation, there was instant feedback, discussion, and validation.

Some male leaders may be upset or reject the idea of this perspective. Candidly, I think this is not any more a conscious decision than the one made when I was assumed to be the administrative support. The point is, just because you're not conscious of it, doesn't mean you get a pass. There are always two or more sides to every story. I get that, and that's precisely the point. All sides and perspectives should be heard.

These stories are not just mine. I've worked with women in leadership roles for many years. I've heard similar stories from them as well. My coaching advice for them is to find someone to echo them, male or female, who will give credit where it's due. I learned to find these confidants on my own. I chose a male leader, whom I respected, and explained this phenomenon. He agreed to echo me, and it changed everything for me. Eventually, enough learning happened around those executive tables that I no longer needed an echo partner.

> "How can we effect change in the world when only half of it is invited or feel welcome to participate in the conversation." (Emma Watson, Actress)

The other coaching advice I offer to female leaders is to learn to do what is traditionally taught to men throughout their lives. That is, to speak up and market your successes, give voice to your gifts, and remind others of your talents. We all have to get past this likability myth. The idea that our competence and performance speak for themselves is, unequivocally, not the case.

In the final two minutes of Brené Brown's 2012 TED talk "Listening to Shame," she dives into this idea that women are expected to be pretty, sexy, and nice. Remember, nice is not kind. It's a self-depreciating version of kind. Kind is saying what needs to be said and being respectful about it. Nice is saying we'll do whatever others want. For you men, the expectations that have been directly or indirectly placed on you are to prioritize work, remain in emotional control, secure a high status, and (sadly) that violence is acceptable. As leaders, we have to be bold enough to pop these thought bubbles wide open. In fact, we have to lead the charge to change the narrative for both genders.

The good news is that more men understand that weakness is not derived from authenticity, the whole of whom they are matters, and violence is never okay. On the other end, women are holding top leadership roles in companies and in communities, but the discrepancy is still widely evident, particularly at the most senior leadership roles. Based on the S&P 500 list posted in January 2019, women held twenty-five (5.0%) of the Chief Executive Officer (CEO) positions at the S&P 500 companies. In 2018, there were twenty-four, and in 2016, there were just twenty. In the very week I wrote this chapter, the 116th Congress of the United States welcomed it's most diverse group to Capitol Hill to date. Change is upon us. As leaders, we must continue to evolve, too.

At the end of it all, it is our job to move the business forward in its mission, leveraging the talents of our staff to bring out the best in all of them. Leaders must hear, see, and appreciate all sides. Understanding there are many different points of view is critical to leading teams successfully. Seeking to understand each perspective is the hard work that leaders must accept and even, dare I say, enjoy. Disagreements don't indicate a lack of understanding on either side. Disagreements are just that–difference of perspectives.

Leading teams is difficult work because you're managing the values, biases, and skill sets within a diverse group of people. Unfortunately in every team, there will be those who don't agree with how you manage differences, conflict, or performance. As the old adage goes, "You can't please everyone." In the next chapter, we'll unpack how to manage those kinds of critics. I call them the invisible critics.

~ 12 ~
FIGHTING THE INVISIBLE CRITIC

THERE ARE CRITICS that reside so high up in the stands that the warriors cannot even see or hear them. They are called invisible critics. As the gladiators of the Roman Empire hyper-focused on what was happening in the center of the arena, they were tuned out to the hecklers and naysayers far enough away to be out of sight and mind. They had enough to worry about as the vicious creatures they were about to fight entered the staging area.

Ironically, in the workplace, these invisible critics are typically found on our secondary teams, among our own staff. They are invisible because, at least initially, we don't know who they are. Unlike in the Roman Colosseum, they are not physically removed from our arena, but they are also not in our direct line of sight or hearing. Unfortunately, those around them (usually other team members) can and do hear their voices. For that reason, invisible critics can be simple irritants, or they may transform into dangerous disruptors of either team unity or, in extreme cases, our leadership careers. What we don't know *can* hurt us.

In order to help us understand how invisible critics operate, I have classified them into three distinct categories.

TEAPOTS

Teapots are the critics who need to blow off steam. They span the continuum from harmless to dangerous, and their primary motivation is frustration. Teapots who complain to other team members about us (as their leader) are reacting in a natural way. In most cases, their behavior is not terribly serious, but it is easier for these individuals to address their frustrations about us with others rather than with us. Honestly, we've all likely been teapots at some point in our careers. We've had leaders we disagreed with, and we took our discontent to the water cooler.

The teapot is typically the most benign of the invisible critics. The more damaging teapots are those who blow off steam with people in strategic positions–our managers, peers, or HR partners, as examples. Overactive teapots can damage teams, and those who vent outside of the team and in strategic areas can, inadvertently, damage our reputations. This is especially true if those strategic people are critics themselves. The environment you create as a leader will go far in mitigating or inflaming the chronic teapots.

There is a saying that has become common in recent years. *What people think about you is none of your business.* This is true to the extent you allow what people think of you to impact your thoughts, feelings and behaviors. I believe the point of this statement is that confidence is a head game, and if we allow negative stuff into our minds, we lose. This is especially true in leadership. While it my feel like it is important to know what is being said, what's more important is how we behave and present ourselves, especially when we find out what is being said. We don't need to seek out the information. It remains our responsibility to stay in control of our heads (protect our thoughts and monitor our assumptions) and play our own game, not the games of others.

We all have light and dark sides. While we can surround ourselves with people who help us be our best selves, in the end, we need to be confident in who we are in order to rise above the noise from the invisible critics.

The goal with teapots is to create the environment where they feel safe to blow off steam. That is the role of the leader. This means we need to make sure we listen without judgment and are open to providing help, clarifying their interpretations, and accepting the feedback with gratitude. I have a friend who always reminds me, "Feedback is a gift." I remind myself, "Gifts are returnable." Here's the thing: Feedback is indeed a gift, but if we honestly listen, digest it, and then believe it isn't applicable to us, then we can return it to the universe. We don't have to hold onto it. Just because someone doesn't believe the truth, doesn't make it false.

While the teapot's choice to vent is a natural thing, there are ways to effectively manage these critics once we do learn about them. The ideal situation is if we've already created an environment in which teapots can come into our offices, blow off steam about something we've done or said, and feel perfectly safe in doing so. Teapots will only come forth if they know we're not going to hold any type of grudge against them. One of the worst things a leader can do is create a culture that feels like silos using words such as, "Don't bring me any bad news." We must show others it's okay to voice their concerns through our behavior, as well. If we stay calm and build rapport with our staff members in the face of frustrating feedback, we will create an inviting culture.

Creating this environment can eliminate most teapot behavior, but at the end of the day, we all need to vent and sometimes, it will be about the leader. When we are the leaders, it is truly none of our business. The open and trusting environment is a difficult one to establish. It takes time, but it's never too late to start. I was only able to accomplish this deep into my own leadership journey, but as emerging leaders reading this book, you now have more insight than I did when I was in your position.

The other end of the spectrum when attempting to manage teapots is if leaders try to change themselves in an effort to become agreeable, accommodating, or nicer in order to stop a teapot from venting. As a reminder, when our goal is to be nice or agreeable, we're not leading to move our business forward in its mission. In leadership, it is not important to be liked. We should strive to be respected and likewise, respect our team members, but liking each other is not the point.

When I first became a Vice President, I was so excited to see other women at the leadership table. I went to my first leadership meeting wide-eyed and giddy–a kid at an amusement park. My personal mission seemed within reach, the one to change the industry in which I worked and give voice to women at all levels. With two other women in high leadership positions alongside me, I thought, *finally, we'll have some influence around our perspective!*

Oh, was I ever disappointed! The two other women didn't talk to me. I felt like I was back in middle school again, and feelings of not being good enough emerged. It was an adult version of girls being mean, and I was the target.

Ironically, I ended up working for both women during two different seasons over the next couple of decades, and each one handled me as a direct report very differently. With one, I could go to her, honestly vent, and feel some satisfaction that I had been heard. She was empathetic and thoughtful. The other woman was a bull in a china shop where no one knew what impulsive and reactive behavior she might exhibit at any given moment. She never created a safe environment for others to be honest with her, so I did a lot of venting to peers.

It's okay to be a teapot once or twice, but peers start to tire of coworkers' frustrations. I had become a Negative Nellie, if you will. I was constantly bitching about the same thing, and I never took the action to change it nor did I let it go. That's when a teapot becomes dangerous. Chronic teapots tend to quit mentally and emotionally. I stopped engaging with others, I became unproductive, I feared for my job, and frustration whispered, "You can't do anything right." At this point, I had many successful years under my belt, but this leader did nothing but chip away at my confidence. My inner critic then fueled more venting, and a relentless cycle emerged. The good news is that somehow, I persevered, and she finally moved on.

Chronic teapots become impediments to our teams' development and team cohesiveness. Our (secondary) teams expect us to see when this starts to happen. They expect us to be omniscient and omnipotent. If Frank is bitching about work, then the assumption is we know about it since Frank works for us. When nothing happens and no change is forthcoming, we lose motivation from everyone.

Eventually, we may be fortunate enough to performance manage chronic teapots out of the business, and the reaction from our teams will be "it's about time." These chronic teapots are invisible critics because they are hard to find. In fact, you may never know they are there. Teapots are way up in the stands, at the water coolers, and in the break rooms, and when you are made aware of them, act quickly to engage (be open and curious), address concerns, and if necessary, start performance management.

NEWSMONGERS

Left to their own behavior, chronic teapots can evolve. Most teapots are not trying to take people down; however, when they continue to vent uninhibited and without the satisfaction of feeling heard, their motives begin to change. They can become newsmongers.

In general, a newsmonger–a gossip with more disparaging motivations–aims to knock others down in an effort feel more powerful or important. Newsmongers talk about things that reduce others' success, importance, or self-worth. They judge, and they do it vocally. You'll find these employees in the outdoor smoking areas, break room, and yes, even in the restrooms. With the influx of technology, it also happens during meetings via instant messaging, with texting tools, and sometimes even in email. They band together and compare notes. These types of people feed off each other, and they become a chronic voice of discontent, always questioning the leaders above them. It takes many years for newsmongers to develop this type of critical personality, and the gossip they spew becomes part of the fabric of who they are.

Believe it or not, there is some good that comes from the newsmongers' behaviors. They create relationships and camaraderie. They establish community, and this is an important part of the workplace, particularly within your secondary team. The challenge is that it's a judgmental community with negative energy that we, as the leaders, must redirect.

I once saw a picture in a store that was meant to be a joke. It said *if you can't say something nice, come sit beside me.* Those people who can't say anything nice are the newsmongers. If they come to your attention, you can help them with coaching, mentoring, or when necessary, even discipline. It is possible to create a culture where this behavior is self-managed. What I mean by that is that peers will hold each other accountable for this behavior and begin to show each other, through their actions, that it is not acceptable. This takes time, and the behavior has to be modeled by the leader. It's the proverbial "walk the talk" scenario.

*   *   *

I had a CEO whom I adored. He was unrehearsed and unpretentious, showing up to work on casual Fridays in blue jeans and a wrinkled and untucked dress shirt. I found this very refreshing for the corporate world. He was truly a casual person, inside and out. I also had a colleague (he was male, though I'm not sure if that matters) who would come up to me every Friday and stir the gossip pot.

"We need to talk to him. He's the CEO! He shouldn't dress that way. It's embarrassing."

My response was always the same. "Don't you think he's a more approachable CEO when he dresses this way? He is establishing a culture of transparency and comfort. It's who he is, and it's the type of company he wants to run."

*   *   *

The higher we move in a corporate setting, the more our decisions and actions are visible. We are on a stage, so to speak. Think of it as being the number one warrior fighting the premiere battle in the arena, the one all the townspeople really come to watch. It means people will start talking.

I was still new in my first leadership role and living in North Carolina. I was still getting used to the weird questions leaders tend to get. If you've been in leadership any length of time, you know what I'm talking about. People, whom I did not know in the company, would stop me and ask the strangest things. "This morning, why did you turn left when leaving the parking lot? Usually, you turn right."

Wow. What the hell? Not only are people curious, but they also expect us to answer their silly questions. As you've learned by now, I'm a bit self-protective. What I wanted to say was, "That's none of your damn business." Instead, I paused and chose wisely. I replied, "I don't recall. Why is it important?" No sensible answer was forthcoming. It would be wonderful if everyone in our homes, communities, and workplaces followed this insight:

> "Let the improvement of yourself keep you so busy that
> you have no time to criticize others." (Roy T. Bennett,
> Author of *The Light of the Heart*)

As leaders, we must accept that people are always going to worry. Their worry and frustration may escalate. Worry turns to judgment. These critics will make assumptions and talk about us behind our backs. Not all "behind the back" talk is negative, but that is not what this is about. Those who talk negatively about you are letting their inner critics rule their hearts and mouths.

Our role as leaders is to be as transparent as possible so that the missing pieces of information are not filled with the worst possible thinking. Of course, we can only wish that people stuck with the silly and direct questions and never escalated to the malicious gossip. Unfortunately, that is not the case. Critics will always think they can do battle in the arena, even though they have no knowledge of what (and whom) we battle against daily. Ironically, they will rarely risk stepping onto the arena floor themselves.

Saboteurs

The truth about filling the center space in any arena is that not everybody we encounter wants us to be successful. In Roman history, entertainment was derived from battle and ultimately, defeat. The people high up in the stands of the Roman Colosseum gleaned feelings of superiority despite their powerless positions by heckling, and sometimes sabotaging, the warriors. It's the age-old endeavor of putting others down or attempting to make them fail, in order to feel better about themselves. These are the saboteurs.

These are the worst of the invisible critics. Unfortunately, there will always be a handful of these types of outer critics in any arena we enter. They seek out satisfaction from our failures. Saboteurs manufacture chaos or insert a crisis into the heart of the workplace to cause harm and destroy relationships. These outer critics' motives include envy, fear, and self-doubt. In the workplace, they could be the jealous peers who feel passed over for promotions, the worried team members who fear for their jobs, or the employees who don't believe in their self-worth or abilities. Their tactics are varied and can include outspoken displeasure at our ideas or recommendations, subtle and personal jibes, distrust, poor attitudes, or even false accusations. At times, they can look like outer critics. The difference is that buried inside them is a real resentment that is driving their behaviors and makes them focused on our failure.

★   ★   ★

Earlier in my career, after my transition from accounting to IT, I moved into a role working as the consultant to the Chief Information Officer (CIO) two levels above my role. I was unaware that one of the other women on the team (let's call her Sandra) felt she had been stripped of her unofficial "top position" when I was assigned high-exposure projects with the CIO. Sandra also happened to be the dominant female and informal leader of the group of women in our department who had become close friends. Unbeknownst to me, her envy had turned to anger because from her perspective, I had usurped her authority. Apparently, Sandra fumed with a rolling boil of hostility aimed directly at me.

Sandra and I both applied for a new leadership role within the department. After the interview process and while the final decision was being made, I left for a two-week vacation with my husband. I was confident about securing the new position. The CIO and I worked well together, and I had experienced much success.

I returned from vacation fully expecting to finalize my promotion only to find this tribe of women, led by Sandra and a couple of the weaker men (politically-speaking), had convinced the CIO I was having an affair with my new leader. They explained it was the reason I was getting the most sought-after projects.

Needless to say, I did not get the promotion, and when I became aware that these lies were the driving force of the decision, I was floored. The acceptance of this group's false testimony without the decency of seeking out my side of the story was like someone throwing cold water on my face.

I scheduled a sit-down with the CIO to gain some clarity and plead my case. I'll never forget his justification: "Where there's smoke, there's fire," he told me. "For that reason, we're going to let this sit for awhile and readdress it in the spring."

I replied, "You can readdress it whenever the hell you want." I proceeded to seek new employment. Later, I would think of an alternate response that I wish I had used– *Yeah, where's there's smoke, there may be fire, but there may also be mirrors.*

Before spring arrived, I left that job and entered the corporate world. I learned there are two ways to exit a company. We can preserve relationships and use the experience and people around us to catapult us into something bigger and better. Or, we can run away with our flamethrowers and burn bridges behind us so that the critics who hoped for (and perhaps planned for) our exits cannot reach us again. With regards to this particular company, I left with my flamethrower fully engaged and no regrets.

I now want to share one of my biggest leadership failures. It was so painful; it took me nearly a year to recover from it. I had turned into such a critic myself that it took yet another year before people stopped referencing it as something I needed to "get over." I refer to it as my "time out" period, and it set my career back by at least three years.

The story began six years before it actually blew up into chaos. I was fairly new to the corporate world. I was an executive project leader, managing our biggest client and biggest contract. I loved the client and the job. I was so skilled at my role, I was asked by my leader to start using my client as a training ground for new project leaders joining the company. I started cycling new hires through the project, and it was great. They were learning so much, and I was getting a lot of help. It was a win-win for everyone involved.

A year goes by, and I started discussing the idea of a reassignment with my leader. If you consult with a customer for too long, you become ineffective. I was there four days every week, and I was ready for a change of scenery. Enter Steve (name changed, of course).

The first time I met Steve, my gut sent up warning flags. *This guy is gonna be a problem.* I pushed these thoughts off, believing I was simply feeling an unwarranted threat. I convinced myself, *You want him to take your place so you can move on, so let it go.* I did, and he did.

Two years later, Steve had left the company, and I was promoted to Vice President. I was looking for someone to head my flagship product solution. I had interviewed almost everyone who applied–both the internal and external candidates. Steve popped up on my radar. He had not had any leadership experience at this time. Candidly, that has never been an issue for me. Everyone has to start somewhere, so the lack of leadership, (specifically hire/fire experience) didn't concern me. I could coach him.

I took Steve through the paces. My leader signed off, and we were off to the races. Then, another reorganization happened. (Do you sense a theme with reorganizations in my career?) I get a new leader. She is someone I had worked with when I was a customer and really enjoyed her. She asked me to run a project that was recently funded. This would mean that someone would need to fill my role. I recommended Steve, and she agreed.

Within a few months, everything started to fall apart. The internal project was completed, and we were in the test phase. Then my leader leaves, and I get a new one. (Yes, again. You can't make this shit up–I swear.) I had a team assigned to the customer and they were not A-players. Steve was the primary supplier of the staff and was absolutely unwilling to send me people who were at the top of their game. He then convinced people on my team to tell me this project was going to fail, and I should dismantle the processes and put them to work where it makes sense–basically to "sell it for parts." I was wounded and angry. I felt betrayed and deceived. In addition, I was not getting support from my new leader. His words were something to the effect of, "I don't understand why you are having so many issues. None of our other customers are having issues like yours."

At this point, I was so far down the rabbit hole of this project–so invested–that I couldn't see that no one was supporting it. In fact, the story my peers had started to tell themselves was that if I were successful on this project, I would end up being their leader.

The customer was hot. I was getting yelled at every time I visited. Everything was falling apart. I didn't know what to do or where to turn. On top of it all, I acquired a new leader. If you are keeping up, that was the fourth in the span of one year. The good news was that he fired Steve. The bad news was he removed me from the leadership team.

As you can imagine, this story is missing a lot of detail and spanned a number of years. My point here is that sometimes saboteurs are especially close to us. I never understood the motivations for Steve's sabotage.

These invisible critics are dangerous, especially as you move up in the leadership arena. The reason is there is less information coming back to you. I instinctively realized Steve had become a critic, but I didn't know how badly my reputation had been damaged until the rug was yanked out. It was like being pulled from the center of the arena without any explanation. I felt contempt and it probably showed. It took me a long time to battle my way back into the leadership arena.

I played a role in this story that was not insignificant. I did not communicate what was happening well. I didn't help people move through the change. I failed to bring them along. From the outside, I looked like I was keeping secrets, not sharing or asking for input. I was not leading well. I had become so invested in the outcome I envisioned for the project, that I failed to see the shifting landscape. These types of critics only succeed if we play their game. I made it easy for them to point from the stands, yell, and create fear, uncertainty, and doubt in what I was doing and in me.

*   *   *

In these cases, my invisible critics–saboteurs–were successful in undermining my relationships. That's what critics do; they taint our relationships and eventually our careers. In his famed speech, Theodore Roosevelt, though speaking about the critics themselves, seems also to warn leaders not to argue or stoop to the level of their critics. "A cynical habit of thought and speech...an intellectual aloofness which will not accept contact with life's realities–all these are marks, not as the possessor would fain to think, of superiority but of weakness." Leaders who are aloof or who avoid the reality of their critics will face consequences. That's what happened to me. Don't let this happen to you. It's important to handle saboteurs quickly, professionally, and intelligently. As a coach, this is my advice:

- Respect what others have to say by critically and actively listening. Everyone wants to feel heard and be seen, but some may not voice that need in an emotionally mature way. No progress can take place until critics feel acknowledged.

- Show up with authenticity. There is no one else like you and the world needs you.
- Communicate and share ideas, solicit input, and change your approach if needed to show others you are flexible.
- Engage and be present with everyone–even the critics.
- Don't argue or try to convince the invisible critics of anything. Avoid reacting with anger, but rather, seek to understand by opening up calm and mature dialogue.
- Trust your instincts. If your gut is saying, *this is going downhill fast*, be ready to do what you need to do to set up boundaries, protect yourself, and possibly look for an exit strategy.
- Find your allies and ask for help. Don't become a critic yourself.

If we do these things, we will be successful. Most people make the assumption that leaders in any arena know everything, so they must know about the invisible critics' behaviors. In reality, there are many instances when leaders don't know who the critics are or what they are saying. Nobody wants to tell leaders (or friends or parents) when others are against them. It's easier for employees to assume leaders already know than it is to confront leaders about the harsh reality. After all, these are difficult conversations to have with people in authority.

People learn early and quickly how you will respond to things you don't like. We can make it an especially difficult conversation to have if our reactions are hostile. We have the choice to lead from authenticity, be brave, and know how to trust our intuition. This will keep invisible critics in the light where they cannot thrive.

~ 13 ~
Triumph in the Arena

LEADERSHIP IS A lifelong journey. It's a journey that compels us to learn about ourselves, others, and perhaps most importantly, one that helps us learn from our failures and lead smarter. Thank you for journeying with me through this book. I hope it was a meaningful and thoughtful experience, one in which you were able to learn from as you read through my own successes and failures.

My specific leadership journey has solidified the philosophy of my coaching business and the content of this book. I have shared my authentic stories of success, but more so, I chose to reveal my failures in an effort to help you take a shortcut and learn from them. Perhaps you also gained a new perspective on failing and can now experience some level of insight from your own experiences. My ultimate hope is you start to live out the lessons and become successful leaders.

Great leaders are not born; they are made. Great leaders live and lead with authenticity and kindness. They learn to disrupt fear-based thinking and be brave, and they discover the need to be curious in every interaction with others. In fact, it's likely that this curiosity is what allows them to move past their fears as they seek out understanding and clarity. Curiosity helps us move forward.

"Around here, however, we don't look backwards for very long. We keep moving forward, opening up new doors and doing new things, because we're curious...and curiosity keeps leading us down new paths." (The Walt Disney Company)

My goal was to help emerging and transitioning leaders navigate their arenas with an armload of strategies and gain a new level of leadership mastery. I hope the content of this book provided you with a fresh arsenal and freed you of the weight critics can put upon you. I hope you are more prepared to get your ass kicked, knowing that winning is in the getting back up. My stories are a testament of how we can get back up and keep fighting. It is a process, and we cannot avoid the difficulties, but we can conquer them.

However, we cannot effect change simply by learning new ways to do things. It takes authentic living to transition into fully "being." We must know our visions, breathe our visions, and live our visions. Otherwise, we cannot communicate our visions. We must take action, engage in the battles, discover our weaknesses, and embrace our failures as gifts of the learning process. As leaders, we are called to push ourselves toward sustainable change. I call this living into being. More precisely, living is the bridge from learning to being. This is the *Learn. Live. Be.* model, and it's based on my own journey as well as this saying from a well-known man:

"You can't solve a problem with the same level of consciousness that created it." (Albert Einstein)

Change. We must wrestle with it to solve problems, grow, and improve. Change moves us from knowing what it is we want to do and traversing the gap between what we want to do and what we are doing.

Not every solution others choose will be right for us. In fact, some of my strategies may not be right for you on your own journey. You could have read any of the thousands of other books on leadership. The mission of this one was to show how trial and error, when paired with belief in self, help us find victory in our arenas.

Our jobs as leaders is to coach people to get to and stay in an optimal state of performance. Growth requires perseverance. If we press forward and choose not to give up during the heat of the battle, we will triumph. My hope is we never lose sight of our ability to succeed, for we can be catalysts for change in every arena we find ourselves.

As a final note on change, there are five discoveries we must make to create lasting change according to Richard Boyatzis, an American organizational theorist. They align well with our tools of the trade. We must discover:

1. Our ideal self and personal vision.
2. Our real self and its comparison to our ideal self so we have the sense of a personal balance sheet.
3. Our learning agenda and a plan.
4. Our ability to practice the desired changes.
5. Our ability to have trusting relationships that will help us learn.

We pass through these discoveries as we enter each new arena. The first and second discoveries relate to self-mastery. The fifth one lends itself to the mastery of our relationships and teams. We're all human. Even the person across from you with whom you're having a great debate or with whom you've experienced distrust is human. We all feel. We all hurt. We all have a desire for growth. We can all be curious and open.

Each arena has its own battles and its own critics. If you define your foundation and hone the four weapons, you will succeed. I do recommend the foundation of bravery and authenticity, but your foundation could be different. Perhaps in your arena, you need to establish kindness and collaboration as the foundational virtues from which to lead and make decisions. Or, you may choose the foundation of transparency and respect. Regardless of what you choose, the weapons remain the same. In each arena, you will need to master self, communication, relationships, and teams.

The truth is that each new level of leadership is it's own arena, and you'll have to revisit those tools, sharpen them with your new perspective and vantage point, and glean new wisdom after each move in the leadership journey. While critics will always be present, they will look different–wearing different masks, using new tactics, and shouting fresh criticisms. The information in this book is cyclical, and as with all good books, you'll learn something new each time you revisit it.

No matter our position, if we go into the arena to build relationships and teams, tackle our critics, and surround our work life with constant openness and curiosity, we will fall down and be covered in mud, dust, and blood (figuratively). It will feel paralyzing, but I encourage you to keep going because it's worth it. You will triumph.

There will be places of doubt, as you read in my stories, but I hope you've learned you can surround yourself with people who will come alongside you during those seasons and breathe confidence–new life–into you. The people who believed in me did that for me, reminding me that I was worthy and good enough to lead in new arenas. It's the reason I was brave enough to leave a twenty-five-year career in senior leadership to start coaching others.

In fact, as my final transparent testimony, my inner critics tried to shake my confidence about becoming an entrepreneur. Most people would never step off a remarkably successful path to pursue something brand new at my age. Doubt. Insecurity. I experienced them both. I knew I must start my journey all over again, including sharpening my weapons. But, I also followed my own advice and surrounded myself with people who believed in me. I relied on them for feedback and help, so I could be better and remember what it was I had learned. When I became stuck (I had moments when I asked myself, "What the f*ck have I done?"), I turned to them.

This book is the most basic form of advice and stories so others who haven't done battle in the leadership arena, are forging their weapons, or are currently struggling in a new arena can grab hold and be successful.

I want to end with the power of choice. Through these stories and strategies, I share the truth that we always have choices. When we understand this, we are empowered to show up. We are empowered to have a voice, stand up for our values, and to fight, flee, or freeze in any situation that warrants a response. I hope you always choose to get back up and lead on.

When we do lead on, we can choose to lead from one of two mindsets–the growth mindset or a fixed mindset. "Over thirty years ago, Carol Dweck and her colleagues became interested in students' attitudes about failure. They noticed that some students rebounded while other students seemed devastated by even the smallest setbacks. After studying the behavior of thousands of children, Dr. Dweck coined the terms fixed mindset and growth mindset to describe the underlying beliefs people have about learning." This theory does not only apply to children. In its very simplest form, adults with fixed mindsets don't believe they can change. They believe that their traits, knowledge, and abilities are fixed. Those with growth mindsets have the ability to change because they believe they can. They continue to hone their skills, improve their talents, and become great.

Marshall Goldsmith, a leadership coach, emphasizes this idea that change is crucial to success in his book called, *What Got You Here Won't Get You There*. The first step on our leadership journeys will not be the same as the second step. Each rung of the proverbial ladder is not as straight of a climb as it seems. We have to learn along the way with that growth mindset in play. Each new leadership role is a whole new arena waiting with those weapons, but perhaps they are forged a little differently.

Brené Brown's arenas are topic-based, such as "love, work, etc." My arenas are the multiple positions in the journey of leadership. We can't master everything we need to know as a front line leader and then expect it all to translate when we move into the role of vice president or president. Likewise, we cannot master leadership in a company of 300 people and expect it to transfer to a company of hundreds of thousands of people. There are different cultures, expectations, challenges, and certainly critics. If we stand on our foundation (bravery and authenticity, in my case) and sharpen our tools with openness and curiosity, we will find victory in the center of the arena. I leave you with song lyrics I believe tie it all together.

> *I'm done being stupid and worried and dramatic,*
> *So I lay down my every disguise.*
> *So if ever I can't see the magic around me,*
> *Please take my hands off my eyes.*
> *I don't know where we're from, but we came here to be.*
> *We came here to be courageous.*

May your leadership journey leave you in admiration of not only how far you've come but in awe of all you can still become.

Final Calls to Action

- Go out there and live and lead authentically.
- Bravely live your learning into being.
- Use this guide as a blueprint for navigating the arena.
- When you reach the center, stay humble, open, and curious.
- Accept and promote change.
- Believe in what is possible.

Live it into being...

NOTES

CHAPTER 1

11. Roosevelt, Theodore. *"Citizenship in a Republic."* Speech at the Sorbonne. Paris, France. 23 April 1910.

11. Brown, Brené. *Daring Greatly: How the Courage to Be Vulnerable Transforms the Way We Live, Love, Parent, and Lead.* Garden City: Avery Publishing, 2015.

CHAPTER 2

17 Brown, Brené. *Rising Strong: How the Ability to Reset Transforms the Way We Live, Love, Parent, and Lead.* New York: Random House Trade Paperbacks, 2017.

17 Roosevelt, Theodore. *"Citizenship in a Republic."* Speech at the Sorbonne. Paris, France. 23 April 1910.

CHAPTER 3

19 **"AFI is the percentage of all news stories..."** Thrall, A. Trevor. "Introducing the American Fear Index." *Cato Institute* 14 September 2017. Accessed 25 June 2018, www.cato.org/blog/introducing-american-fear-index.

20 **"If you think that the society around you expects courage..."** Stearns, Peter N. *American Fear: The Causes and Consequences of High Anxiety*. Amazon Digital Services LLC: 2012. Kindle file.

20 **Almost half (41%) of employees...** Folk, Jim and Marilyn, BScN. "Anxiety Effects on Society Statistics." *AnxietyCentre* 25 April 2017. Accessed 11 July 2018, https://www.anxietycentre. com/anxiety-statistics-information.shtml.

20 Steinberg, Scott. *Make Change Work for You: 10 Ways to Future-Proof Yourself, Fearlessly Innovate, and Succeed Despite Uncertainty.* Rego Park: Gildan Media, LLC, 2015.

22 **"In the war for fans..."** Rothman, Lily. "Why Americans Are More Afraid Than They Used to Be." *Time* 06 January 2016. Accessed 18 June 2018, http://time.com/4158007/american-fear-history/.

23 **"Authenticity has been linked to..."** Williams, David K. "15 Things Highly Authentic People Don't Do." *Lifehack* 28 Feb 2017. Accessed 16 Aug 2018, www.lifehack.org/articles/communication/15-things-highly-authentic-people-dont. html.

24 **"...authenticity is not based on only..."** Usheroff, Roz. "The Chameleon Effect: Maintaining Authenticity While Adapting." *The Remarkable Leader* 13 Jan 2015. Accessed 22 Aug 2018, www.remarkableleader.wordpress.com/2015/01/13/the-chameleon-effect-maintaining-authenticity-while-adapting/.

24 **"I see being a chameleon as someone..."** Usheroff, Roz. *The Future of You-Creating Your Enduring Brand.* Palm Beach: Motivated Publishing Studios, 2013.

CHAPTER 5

25 Roosevelt, Theodore. *"Citizenship in a Republic."* Speech at the Sorbonne. Paris, France. 23 April 1910.

29 **"The ultimate measure..."** Inam, H. "Martin Luther King On Leadership: 10 Quotes For A Changing World." *Forbes* 04 April 2018. Accessed 03 March 2019, www.forbes.com/sites/ hennainam/2018/04/04/martin-luther-king-on-leadership-ten-quotes-for-a-changing-world/#587495125c88.

31 Rath, Tom. *StrengthsFinder 2.0.* Washington, D.C.: Gallup Press Publishing, 2007.

32 **VIA Character Strengths and Virtues** VIA Institute on Character. (n.d.). Our mission. Retrieved November 1, 2018, from www.viacharacter.org/www/Character.

35 Brown, Brené. *Daring Greatly: How the Courage to Be Vulnerable Transforms the Way We Live, Love, Parent, and Lead.* Garden City: Avery Publishing, 2015.

CHAPTER 6

36 Roosevelt, Theodore. *"Citizenship in a Republic."* Speech at the Sorbonne. Paris, France. 23 April 1910.

37 **"Blind spots can be..."** Levin, Marissa. "The Top 10 Leadership Blind Spots, and 5 Ways to Turn Them Into Strengths." *Inc.* 13 July 2017. Accessed 02 Nov 2018, www. inc.com/marissa-levin/the-top-10-leadership-blind-spots-and-5-ways-to-tu.html.

39 Goleman, Daniel. *Emotional Intelligence: Why It Can Matter More Than IQ.* London: Bloomsbury Publishing, 1995.

39 **"The term was introduced into mainstream culture…"**
The Emotional Intelligence Institute. Green, Rachel. Mayor and Salovey Model of Emotional Intelligence. Accessed 02 Feb 19, www.theeiinstitute.com/what-is-emotional-intelligence/4-mayer-and-salovey-model-of-emotional-intelligence.html.

CHAPTER 7

43 This contains my interpretations of the copyrighted work of Bruce D. Schneider & the Institute for Professional Excellence in Coaching (iPEC)

45 Carson, Rick. *Taming Your Gremlin: A Surprisingly Simple Method for Getting Out of Your Own Way.* Fort Mill: Quill-House Publishing, 2003 (rev).

46 Ruiz, Don Miguel. *The Four Agreements.* San Rafael: Amber-Allen Publishing, 1997.

CHAPTER 8

49 **"In fact, most neuroscientists would agree…"** Hwang, Victor, W. "What's Better for Business: Logic or Emotion? Answers from Neuroscience." *Forbes* 13 March 2013. Accessed 02 Dec 2018, www.forbes.com/sites/victorhwang/2013/03/27/whats-better-for-business-logic-or-feelings-answers-from-neuroscience/#6840a1b0199b.

52 Mcleod, S. "Maslow's Hierarchy of Needs." *Simply Psychology,* 2019, https://www.simplypsychology.org/maslow.html.

CHAPTER 9

55 **"In fact, 50% of workers..."** Lister, Kate. "Telecommuting Trend Data (Updated July 2018)." *Global Workplace Analytics* March 2016. Accessed 20 Dec 2018, www.globalworkplaceanalytics.com/telecommuting-statistics.

56 **"In a keynote speech..."** Carnegie, Dale. *How to Win Friends and Influence People.* New York: Pocket Books Publishing, 1998.

57 **"In fact, Gallup completed a recent study..."** Mann, Annamarie. "Why We Need Best Friends at Work." *Gallup* 15 Jan 2018. Accessed 17 Feb 2019, www.gallup.com/workplace/236213/why-need-best-friends-work.aspx.

58 Lencioni, Patrick. *The Five Dysfunctions of a Team: A Leadership Fable.* San Francisco: Jossey-Bass Wiley Publishing, 2002.

CHAPTER 10

64 **"Realize it's your job..."** Patterson, K., et. al. (2011) *Crucial Conversations: Tools for Talking When Stakes are High (2nd Edition).* New York, NY: McGraw-Hill Education.

65 Goleman, Daniel. *Emotional Intelligence: Why It Can Matter More Than IQ.* London: Bloomsbury Publishing, 1995.

66 Fickett, Lloyd. *The Collaborative Way: A Story About Engaging the Mind and Spirit of a Company.* LF&A Publishing, 1996.

66 Lencioni, Patrick. *Silos, Politics and Turf Wars: A Leadership Fable About Destroying the Barriers That Turn Colleagues Into Competitors.* San Francisco: Jossey-Bass Wiley Publishing, 2006.

CHAPTER 11

68 **"The Center for Creative Leadership published..."** Gentry, W.A., Logan, P., & Tonidandel, S. (2014). *Understanding the Leadership Challenges of First-Time Leaders: Strengthening Your Leadership Pipeline* [White paper]. Retrieved from www.ccl.org.

73 Brown, Brené. *Rising Strong: How the Ability to Reset Transforms the Way We Live, Love, Parent, and Lead.* New York: Random House Trade Paperbacks, 2017.

74 **"Age plays a colossal role...."** Dimock, Michael. "Defining Generations: Where Millenials End and Generation Z Begins." *Pew Research Center* 17 Jan 2017. Accessed 15 Feb. 2019, www.pewresearch.org/topics/generations–and–age/.

75 [**Generation Chart**] Dimock, Michael. "Defining Generations: Where Millenials End and Generation Z Begins." *Pew Research Center* 17 Jan 2017. Accessed 15 Feb. 2019, www.pewresearch.org/topics/generations–and–age/.

76 [**"Managers Use More Positive Words..."** Chart] Smith, David G., Rosenstein, Judith E., & Nikolov, Margaret C. "The Different Words We Use to Describe Male and Female Leaders." *Harvard Business Review.* Harvard Business Publishing, 25 May 2018. Accessed 31 Dec. 2018, www.hbr.org/2018/05/the-different-words-we-use-to-describe-male-and-female-leaders.

76 **"Leadership attributes..."** Smith, David G., Rosenstein, Judith E., & Nikolov, Margaret C. "The Different Words We Use to Describe Male and Female Leaders." *Harvard Business Review.* Harvard Business Publishing, 25 May 2018. Accessed 31 Dec. 2018, www.hbr.org/2018/05/

the-different-words-we-use-to-describe-male-and-female-leaders.

76 **"Even when minimally prepared..."** Gannon, D. "How Men and Women Differ in the Workplace." *The Fiscal Times.* The Fiscal Times Media Group, LLC, 25 May 2012. Accessed 08 Feb 2019, http://www.thefiscaltimes.com/Articles/2012/05/25/How-Men-and-Women-Differ-in-the-Workplace.

76 Craver, Charles B., "Negotiation Styles: The Impact on Bargaining Transactions." Journal of Dispute Resolution (in italics), Vol. 48, April 2003; GWU Legal Studies Research Paper No. 328; GWU Law School Public Law Research Paper No. 328, www.ssrn.com/abstract=1003448.

79 Brown, Brené. "Listening to Shame." TED, March 2012, www.ted.com/talks/brene_brown_listening_to_shame.

79 **"Based on the S&P 500..."** "Women CEOs of the S&P 500." *Catalyst.* 24 January 2019. Web. 15 Feb 2019. www.catalyst.org/research/women-ceos-of-the-sp-500/.

79 **"In 2018, there were twenty-four..."** Mejia, Z. "Just 24 Female CEOs Lead the Companies on the 2018 Fortune 500— Fewer Than Last Year." *Make It.* CNBC, 21 May 2018. Accessed 17 Feb 2019, www.cnbc.com/2018/05/21/2018s-fortune-500-companies-have-just-24-female-ceos.html.

79 Sola, K. "There are Just 20 Women CEOs of S&P 500 Companies. Here's How Much They Make." *Forbes* 06 May 2016. Accessed 17 Feb 2019, www.forbes.com/sites/katiesola/2016/05/06/there-are-just-20-women-ceos-in-sp-500-companies-heres-how-much-they-make/#70bd4fdcf31e.

CHAPTER 12

87   Roosevelt, Theodore. *"Citizenship in a Republic."* Speech at the Sorbonne. Paris, France. 23 April 1910.

CHAPTER 13

89   **"We must discover..."** Boyatzis, R. "The Five Stages of Intentional Change Theory." *Key Step Media* 21 Feb 2017. Accessed 05 Feb. 2019, www.keystepmedia.com/intentional-change-theory/.

90   **"Over thirty years ago..."** www.mindsetworks.com/science/ (2017) Accessed 05 Feb. 2019.

90   Goldsmith, Marshall. *What Got You Here Won't Get You There.* Bluffton: MJF Publishing, 2014.

91   **"I'm done being stupid..."** Cloud Cult. Lyrics to "Through the Ages." *The Seeker.* Concept Indie Album. 12 Feb 2016. CD.

About the Author

Marimac– is an accomplished Senior Executive with more than 25 years of success. She is the Founder & CEO of Learn.Live.Be., a business focused on getting sustainable results for individuals, teams, and organizations through coaching, mentoring, education, and consulting. She holds a Master of Business Administration (MBA) Degree from the University of North Carolina–Wilmington. In addition, she is a Project Management Professional (PMP), Certified Professional Coach (CPC) through iPEC, and a Certified Happiness Trainer.

★　　★　　★

Giving back to the community is an integral part of Marimac's life. She serves as a Board Member for MedPower, a provider of cloud-hosted, custom SaaS e-learning solutions for the healthcare industry. She also sits on the Board of Empowered Girls of North Carolina, Inc. a nonprofit whose mission is to enhance the quality of girls' lives through programs focused on integrity, respect, and self-worth.

For more information, visit www.LearnLiveBe.com.